W9-AQF-396

WITHDRAWN

DON QUIXOTE: HERO OR FOOL?

A Study in Narrative Technique

by John J. Allen

UNIVERSITY OF FLORIDA PRESS / GAINESVILLE

EDITORIAL COMMITTEE

Humanities Monographs

T. WALTER HERBERT, *Chairman*
Professor of English

G. PAUL MOORE
Professor of Speech

CHARLES W. MORRIS
Professor of Philosophy

REID POOLE
Professor of Music

C. A. ROBERTSON
Professor Emeritus of English

MELVIN E. VALK
Professor of German

AUBREY L. WILLIAMS
Professor of English

COPYRIGHT © 1969 BY THE BOARD OF
COMMISSIONERS OF STATE INSTITUTIONS
OF FLORIDA

Second Printing, 1971

LIBRARY OF CONGRESS
CATALOG CARD No. 71-625420
ISBN 0-8130-0268-0

PRINTED BY STORTER PRINTING COMPANY
GAINESVILLE, FLORIDA

CONTENTS

For Tulia

INTRODUCTION

The problem of the reader's attitude toward Don Quixote is perhaps unparalleled in the history of literature, both in duration and extent. The following, by Oscar Mandel, is the most concise of several attempts to summarize the conflicting views: "From the first days in the eighteenth century when *Don Quixote* ceased to be regarded as a mere satire against romances of chivalry, students of the novel have tended to join one of two critical schools, depending on their interpretation of the role played by the knight. A 'soft' school regards Don Quixote as the hero as well as the protagonist of the novel. . . . On the mild side, this view underlines the persistent and invincible sublimity of Don Quixote's motivation and contrasts it with the pedestrian character of the novel's sane folk. On the extreme side, it establishes an analogy with Christ."[1] Mandel places Auden, Unamuno, Bonilla, Rubio, Casella, Ortega y Gasset, Schelling, Menéndez Pidal, and Castro within this group. Helmut Hatzfeld, in another summary, includes Caballero Calderón, García Bacca, Azorín, Babelon, and Ayala in a comparable group,[2] and a third study, by Lienhard Bergel, similarly categorizes Schiller, Novalis, the Schlegels, Byron, Grillparzer, Nietzsche, Vossler, Pfandl, Spitzer, and Thomas Mann.[3]

Mandel continues: "Hardheaded readers who distrust *Schwärmerei* have steadily opposed all these interpretations.

1. "The Function of the Norm in *Don Quixote*," *Modern Philology*, LV (February, 1958), 154-55.
2. "Results from *Quijote* Criticism since 1947," *Anales Cervantinos*, II (1952), 131-32.
3. "Cervantes in Germany," in *Cervantes Across the Centuries*, eds. Angel Flores and M. J. Benardete (New York, 1947), pp. 321 ff.

Don Quixote remains for them, in spite of his nobility, the butt of the satire." In this group, according to Mandel, belong Hegel, Heine, Bell, Bickermann, Parker, Palacios and Mandel himself. Certainly Hatzfeld and René Girard[4] are other important representatives of this school. The apparent paradox which has given rise to this split in opinion has been succinctly put by Lester Crocker: "On the one hand, Cervantes announces his subject as a satire; Don Quijote is a failure, Cervantes mocks him and disapproves of him (therefore for some making him a villain or anti-hero). On the other hand, Don Quijote embodies the great spiritual force of human aspirations, and Cervantes presents him as superior in moral fibre to the people who flout him."[5]

Historically, the process of divergent critical opinion appears to have been somewhat more complex than the development of a simple dichotomy of viewpoint, even if one allows the oversimplification involved in a division into those "for" and those "against" Don Quixote. Cervantes' first public saw in *Don Quixote* only a book of entertainment, a parody.[6] The second stage seems to have been one of *identification* with Don Quixote in his folly. Motteux could say, in 1700, that "every man has something of Don Quixote in his *Humour*, some darling Dulcinea of his Thoughts, that sets him very often upon mad Adventures."[7] Dr. Johnson remarked, in 1750, that "very few readers, amidst their mirth or pity, can deny that they have admitted visions of the same kind. . . . When we pity him, we reflect on our own disappointments; and when we laugh, our hearts inform us that he is not more ridiculous

4. *Mensonge romantique et vérité romanesque* (Paris, 1961), pp. 11 ff; translated as *Deceit and Desire in the Novel: Self and Other in Literary Structure*, by Yvonne Freccero (Baltimore, 1965).

5. *"Don Quijote*, Epic of Frustration," *Romanic Review*, XLII (1951), 177-88.

6. Angel Valbuena Prat, *Historia de la literatura española* (Barcelona, 1937), II, 75; cf. Friedrich Schürr, "Cervantes y el romanticismo," *Anales Cervantinos*, I (1951), 43, and Manuel García Puertas, *Cervantes y la crisis del renacimiento español* (Montevideo, 1962), p. 25.

7. Peter Motteux' Preface to his translation, quoted in Edwin Knowles, "Cervantes and English Literature," in *Cervantes Across the Centuries*, pp. 280-81.

than ourselves, except that he tells what we have only thought."[8] Then, though before Schiller the eighteenth century in Germany "had ventured only timidly to find anything praiseworthy in Don Quixote's dreams,"[9] commentary from England indicates that by mid-century the shift to idealization had already begun. In 1739, a friend of Pope's seemed to him "so very a child in true Simplicity of Heart, that I love him; as he loves Don Quixote, for the most Moral and Reasoning Madman in the world."[10] In 1754, finally, Sarah Fielding could say: "To travel through a whole work only to laugh at the chief companion allotted us, is an insupportable burthen. And we should imagine that the reading of that incomparable piece of humor left us by Cervantes, can give but little pleasure to those persons who can extract no other entertainment or emolument from it than laughing at Don Quixote's reveries, and sympathizing in the malicious joy [of his tormentors]. ... That strong and beautiful representation of human nature, exhibited in Don Quixote's madness in one point, and extraordinary good sense in every other, is indeed very much thrown away on such readers as consider him only as the object of their mirth."[11]

Without considering eccentric or purely individual response, then, the range of reader attitude toward Don Quixote seems to include derisive laughter, identification, pity, and admiration. Faced with this perplexing diversity of attitudes, it is tempting to suspend judgment by taking refuge in the idea of the god-like ambiguity or impartiality of Cervantes, or to decide, with Américo Castro, that to Cervantes "the actions, attitudes, or opinions of each character do not appear as good or bad, clever or stupid, judged from without."[12] But recent work on ethical orientation in the novel makes such an evasion

8. *The Rambler*, No. 2, also quoted in Knowles.

9. Bergel, "Cervantes in Germany," p. 321.

10. Alexander Pope, *Correspondence*, IV, 208, quoted in Stuart Tave, *The Amiable Humorist* (Chicago, 1960), p. 154.

11. *The Cry*, III, 120-24; also quoted in Tave.

12. "Incarnation in *Don Quixote*," trans. Zenia Sacks Da Silva [from "La estructura del *Quijote*"], in *Cervantes Across the Centuries*, p. 144.

of judgment difficult, for it now seems established that "a novelist not merely may but must subtly control our feelings about the characters, acts, and thoughts represented at each stage of the novel if it is to have a coherent effect."[13]

This, then, will be the object of the present study: to elucidate Cervantes' devices of disclosure of the proper ethical perspective toward Don Quixote, those "formal variables which affect our reactions to characters, their acts and thoughts,"[14] with the goal being not simply to establish yet another, more sophisticated judgment of Don Quixote, but rather to see how so many apparently conflicting judgments have arisen, and to attempt to see the various bases for these judgments as parts of a coherent and integral interpretation.

Chapter 1 is concerned with the question of the reader-author-character relationship, and examines authorial omniscience, suppression or omission of information, and reliability, in order to judge authorial commentary on Don Quixote and the degree to which the reader can depend upon the author in his account of the knight's activities. Chapter 2 focuses on Don Quixote's defeats, stressing the devices of disclosure in the immediately surrounding context which determine the reader's desires and expectations as to the outcome of each encounter. Chapter 3 discusses a number of stylistic devices which affect the reader's judgment of Don Quixote. In Chapter 4 several distinct levels of fiction in *Don Quixote* are identified, and the violation of verisimilitude in Part II is discussed in its relationship to the reader's judgment of Don Quixote's delusions. Chapter 5 concludes the work with a judgment of Don Quixote.

The appearance of Volume IV of Otis Green's *Spain and the Western Tradition* coincided with the conclusion of Chapter 2 of this study. It contains a wonderfully succinct and perceptive presentation of the effects of the techniques out-

13. Sheldon Sacks, *Fiction and the Shape of Belief* (Berkeley, 1967), p. 65. Another important recent contribution to the problem of the role and the devices of the narrator is Wayne Booth, *The Rhetoric of Fiction* (Chicago, 1961).

14. Sacks, p. 65.

lined here, and lends force to the conclusions here adduced as to the ethical orientation of the reader by Cervantes. Insofar as this investigation is successful, it examines *how* Cervantes achieves the effects which Professor Green, building on a "luminous article" ("The Concept of Reality in *Don Quijote*," by Alexander Parker), also basic to this study, has so lucidly described.[15] In any work on Cervantes the debt to previous criticism is enormous, and I shall not attempt to acknowledge specifically this debt beyond what will be obvious from the notes.

I must express my profound gratitude to Professor Mack Singleton of the University of Wisconsin, who initiated me in the study of Cervantes and *Don Quixote*, to Professors Alfred Hower and Murray Lasley for their critical reading of my manuscript, to the Humanities Council of the College of Arts and Sciences at the University of Florida for a grant under which much of the study was written, and to the Krahe Schmid family of "Los Cerrillos," near Argamasilla de Alba, for an inspiring sojourn in La Mancha.

15. Otis H. Green, *Spain and the Western Tradition: The Castilian Mind in Literature from "El Cid" to Calderón*, IV (Madison, 1966), 60-73.

1. THE "AUTHORS"

Don Quixote is really the first important
novel using the self-conscious narrator.

Wayne Booth, "The Self-Conscious
Narrator in Comic Fiction before
Tristram Shandy," *PMLA,* LXVII
(1952), 165.

The isolation and judgment of authorial commentary in *Don Quixote* is greatly complicated by the profusion of fictional intermediaries which Cervantes has interposed between himself and the events of the story, especially since, as George Haley points out, "each of the intermediaries who work at telling and transmitting Don Quijote's story functions, at the same time, as a critical reader of a previous version of that story."[1]

Cervantes' fictional self, the "second author,"[2] is the reader's immediate source for the entire narration. *His* sources for the first eight chapters are several and disparate; "there is some difference of opinion among those who have written on the subject" (25-26), and at times he must have recourse to "the most likely conjectures" (26). This fictional Cervantes is not a simple copyist, but a dedicated researcher who bases part of his narration on "what I have read in the annals of La Mancha" (32). These sources dwindle, by Chapter VIII, to a single author who, in the middle of Don Quixote's battle with the valorous Biscayan, in turn exhausts *his* sources, "excusing himself upon the ground that he has been unable to find anything else in writing concerning the exploits

1. "The Narrator in *Don Quijote*: Maese Pedro's Puppet Show," *Modern Language Notes*, 80 (1965), 148.
2. *The Ingenious Gentleman Don Quixote de la Mancha*, trans. Samuel Putnam (New York: Viking Press, 1949), p. 69. Subsequent references are to this edition. Italics within quotations from *Don Quixote* are mine throughout, and departures from the Putnam translation, at times for accuracy, at other times for precision, are also mine, and are in brackets and identified by an asterisk preceding the page reference, e.g., (*665).

11

of Don Quixote" (69).[3] Cervantes' diligence in seeking further accounts is rewarded in Chapter IX by the discovery of the Arabic manuscript of Cid Hamete Benengeli, which consists of the remainder of Part I, and which apparently begins precisely where the former fragments ended, since early doubts about Don Quixote's name and the order of events (43) are not resolved, and "in the first of the books [of Cid Hamete] there was a very lifelike picture of the battle between Don Quixote and the Biscayan" (72). Between Cervantes and Cid Hamete's manuscript stands the Moorish translator, who has access to the text itself plus certain marginal notes, some "in Hamete's own handwriting" (665), others apparently not: "This Dulcinea del Toboso, so often referred to, is said to have been the best hand at salting pigs of any woman in all La Mancha" (72).

The end of Part I (1605) coincides with the end of Cid Hamete's manuscript, and the only indication of Don Quixote's future activities is "the tradition, handed down in La Mancha, to the effect that in the course of this third expedition he went to Saragossa . . ." (459). This piece of information, by an ironic twist which Cervantes must certainly have appreciated, could only have had its source in Avellaneda's spurious second part (1614), for in the authentic Part II (1615), based upon another manuscript by Cid Hamete about which the reader is given no information, the protagonist refuses to set foot in Saragossa (898). Cervantes thus represents himself as dependent upon Cid Hamete, a Moorish translator, marginal notes, hearsay and oral tradition, other unspecified authors, and the annals of La Mancha. These are the authors and sources whose relative omniscience and reliability must be investigated before a judgment can be made concerning authorial commentary and the ethical orientation of the reader.

---

3. This explanation still seems the most acceptable despite George Haley's postulation of a "shadowy figure who materializes at the end of Chapter VIII to join the first author's fragment to the second author's contribution . . ." (p. 148).

THE TRUTH

In the first eight chapters, some, at least, of the sources upon which the fictional Cervantes depends are omniscient. Despite the differences indicated above among these sources, the composite account records the inner thoughts of the characters, and reproduces textually Don Quixote's words, when, for example, he is "talking to himself" (31). Nevertheless, the account surrounds with vague reservations certain details which are later to become extremely significant: "*As the story goes*, there was a very good-looking farm girl who lived near by, with whom he had once been smitten, although *it is generally believed* that she never knew or suspected it" (29).

After Chapter VIII, Cervantes depends almost entirely upon Cid Hamete's manuscript, mediated through the Moorish translator. The exceptions to this total dependence, apart from the note alluding to Dulcinea's culinary talents mentioned above, are two:

> It has become a tradition handed down from father to son [that] the author of this veracious chronicle even wrote a number of special chapters on the subject [of the friendship between Rocinante and the gray] (*581).

> They say that in the original version of the history it is stated that the interpreter did not translate the present chapter as Cid Hamete had written it (788).

Cid Hamete's account, like the sources of Chapters I-VIII, is omniscient: "[Sancho] began talking to himself, as follows . . . " (567); "at this point a thought occurred to [Don Quixote]" (211), and this is reflected in Sancho's comments on learning of the publication of the Moorish enchanter's history: "And he says that they mention me in it, under my own name, Sancho Panza, and the lady Dulcinea del Toboso as well, along with things that happened to us when we were alone together. I had to cross myself, for I could not help wondering how the one who wrote all those things down could have come to know about them" (525). But there are curious intermittent limitations on Cid Hamete's omniscience. At times, he is dependent upon subsequent information:

> The only [verses] that proved to be legible were the following . . . (211).

> which was the fact, as he himself afterward admitted (212)

> Even Sancho Panza wept, although, as he said afterward, it was only at finding that Dorotea was not as he had thought Queen Micomicona (330).

> [*It is considered certain*] that at the time of his death [*they say*] he retracted what he had said (*666).

At others, Cid Hamete shows himself dependent upon inference or conjecture:[4]

> Had the knight's mounting wrath permitted him to do so, it is my opinion that he would have laughed at the sight (128).

> [From these tears and this noble resolve on the part of Sancho Panza the author of this history deduces that he must have been well bred] (*153).

At other times, Cid Hamete shows himself dependent upon other sources for his account:

> It was commonly said of the good lass that she never made such a promise without keeping it (117).

> It is said that he had suffered for many years from a kidney ailment (621).

> a song which the cousin proceeded to memorize and which [they say] went like this (*669)

> It is the general belief that there was only the one in front to hold up the breeches (900).

Finally, on certain occasions Cid Hamete seems to have been excluded from events, although he may be aware of what transpired:

---

4. See also the examples of authorial conjecture in Richard L. Predmore, *The World of "Don Quixote"* (Cambridge, Mass., 1967), pp. 80-81.

Here, Cid Hamete inserts a parenthesis in which he swears by Mohammed that to have seen the two walking hand in hand like this from the door to the bed he would have given the better of the two cloaks that he had (819).

THE WHOLE TRUTH

In general, despite Cid Hamete's request that he be praised "not for what he writes, but for what he has refrained from writing" (789), the reader must incline to the opinion of Cervantes: "Really and truly, all those who enjoy such histories as this one ought to be grateful to Cid Hamete, its original author, for the pains he has taken in setting forth every detail of it, leaving out nothing, however slight, but making everything very clear and plain. He describes thoughts, reveals fancies, answers unasked questions, clears up doubts, and settles arguments. In short, he satisfies on every minutest point the curiosity of the most curious" (764).

Very little is excluded from the main thread of the narrative. Except for a day and a night on the way to El Toboso, which Don Quixote and Sancho passed "without anything happening to them worthy of note" (561), six days on the way home at the end of Part I (458), six with the duke and duchess (735), two on the banks of the Ebro on the way to Saragossa, and more than six before meeting Roque Guinart "without anything happening to him that is worthy of being set down in writing" (689, 899), the reader is scarcely without a detailed account of the protagonist's activities. The space of a day and a half near the end of the novel "with nothing occurring worthy of note" serves as ironic background to the concessive clause full of significance for the conquered knight: "Save for the fact that Sancho completed his task [of disenchanting Dulcinea]" (977). The "long and agreeable conversation, in the course of which Sancho made so many droll remarks, and mischievous ones as well" to the duke and duchess, is also omitted, and there are times when Cid Hamete decides to omit something deliberately, such as the place in La Mancha which Cid Hamete "was unwilling to designate exactly" (987), or the "special chapters" on the two animals (581) mentioned above.

In addition, we know that the translator has intervened more than might be expected in the transmission of the material. He "passed over [the description of Don Diego's house] and other similar details in silence, since they did not fit in with the chief purpose of the chronicle" (*621), and he took the liberty of omitting Cid Hamete's lament at having restricted himself to the story of Don Quixote and Sancho, since "he has sufficient ability and intelligence to take the entire universe for his theme if he so desired" (789).[5]

Despite the infrequency of such omissions and suppressions, scarcely a handful in a novel of a thousand pages, the impression is strong that there is much more to the story than the reader is permitted to witness. The allusions to other sources, differences of opinion, and omitted chapters are responsible, in part, for this impression, but other resources of technique are brought to bear for the same effect. Joaquín Casalduero has mentioned the unwritten chapter of conversation between Sancho and Teresa which must have preceded the former's masterfully presented demand for a fixed wage in Chapter VII of Part II,[6] and there are other, more subtle examples. In Part II, Chapter V, Sancho has just informed Teresa, in a most confused manner, that he and Don Quixote are about to set out on a third sally: " 'Listen to me, Sancho,' his wife replied. 'Ever since you [became a member of a knight-errant], you've been talking in such a roundabout way that there's no understanding you' " (*539). With a single word, "member," Teresa brings to the reader's mind the exchange between Sancho and Don Quixote three chapters earlier, demonstrates the linguistic influence of the knight on his squire, and points to an unrecorded conversation between herself and Sancho. The passage from Chapter II is as follows:

5. This passage would seem to challenge Wayne Booth's claim for the originality of Fielding in a similar passage, as asserted in "The Self-Conscious Narrator in Comic Fiction before *Tristram Shandy*," *PMLA*, LXVII (1952), 179.

6. *Sentido y forma del "Quijote"* (Madrid, 1966), p. 241.

"I mean," said Don Quixote, "that when the head suffers, all the other members suffer also. Being your master and lord, I am your head, and you, being my servant, are a part of me; and so it is that the evil which affects me must likewise affect you and your pain must be my own."

"It may be so," Sancho answered, "but I know that when they were blanketing me, as a member, my head was on the other side of the wall, watching me fly through the air, without feeling any pain whatever" (523).

Another device of Cervantes' narrative technique, which relates both to omniscience and to the problem of reliability, consists in posing alternative possibilities (almost always two) for the designation of an object, motivation of an action, or explanation of an event. This aspect, brilliantly expounded by both Castro[7] and Spitzer,[8] is basic to their respective interpretations of the novel, and culminates in the famous "basin-helmet" neologism created by Sancho in Chapter XLIV of Part I. The range of the use of this device in the novel covers a broad spectrum. At one pole are ridiculous distinctions such as the following:

At this juncture, whether it was the cool of the morning which was coming on, or something laxative he had eaten at supper, or—which is most likely—merely a necessity of nature, Sancho felt the will and desire to do that which no one else could do for him (151).

three ass-colts or fillies—the author is not specific on this point (568)

five or six buckets of water (there is some difference of opinion as to the exact number) (621)

oak or cork trees (on this point Cid Hamete is not as precise as he usually is) (899).

the trunk of a beech—or it may have been a cork tree, for Cid Hamete Benengeli is not definite on the point (954)

7. "Incarnation in *Don Quixote*" [from "La palabra escrita y el *Quijote*"], p. 160.
8. Leo Spitzer, "Linguistic Perspectivism in the *Don Quijote*," in *Linguistics and Literary History* (New York, 1962), pp. 59-60.

17

More significant is the disturbing uncertainty about Don Quixote's real name, and the device at its most significant involves its application to important occurrences in Don Quixote's life, such as the relationship between the knight and Dulcinea, the truth of his account of the episode of the Cave of Montesinos, and the cause of his death.

Despite the considerable body of critical commentary on this device, some of it excellent, it seems necessary to discuss it here in its full range of variation, emphasizing its significance as a narrative device, and its bearing upon the issue of authorial reliability. There is, of course, on the most superficial level, a parody of the pseudo-historical references to variant sources in the novels of chivalry. This mock illusion of historicity was undoubtedly the motivation behind the five examples quoted above. At times the option seems to be introduced simply to leave things a little unclear, particularly concerning the effects of Don Quixote's actions. After Marcela's eloquent self-exoneration in Chapter XIV, Part I, Don Quixote forbids anyone to follow her into the woods. The author follows the knight's injunction with this comment: "Whether it was due to Don Quixote's threats or because Ambrosio now told them that they should finish doing the things which his good friend had desired should be done, no one stirred from the spot. . . " (106). The most interesting aspect of this "elusive style," as Castro has called it, for the investigation of narrative technique and authorial reliability is, however, not simply the existence of alternatives at different points in the narrative, but the way in which these alternatives are proposed in certain cases. The author does not say: "His name was either Quijada, Quejana, Quijana, Quesada, or Quijano." The presentation is as follows: "They will try to tell you that his surname was Quijada or Quesada —there is some difference of opinion among those who have written on the subject—but according to the most likely conjectures we are to understand that it was really Quejana" (25-26). Though uncertain, the conclusion seems to be final: Quejana. It is thus rather disconcerting to encounter the following passage four pages later: "He had made up his mind that he was henceforth to be known as Don Quixote, which, *as has been stated,* has led the authors of this veracious history to assume that his real name must undoubtedly have been Quijada, and not Quesada as others would have it" (29). At this point the reader registers the new conclusion: Quijada (*undoubtedly*), but with a vague sense of unease and confusion proportionate to his recollection of the author's previous "likely conjectures." The next option arises in Chapter V, when Don Quixote meets his neighbor Pedro Alonso, who addresses him as " 'Señor Quijana' (for such must have been Don Quixote's real name when he was in his right senses . . .)" (48). Much later, Don Quixote gives two solutions himself, one when he mentions Gutierre Quijada, "from whom I am descended in the direct male line" (440), and the other at the end of Part II: "I am no longer Don Quixote de la Mancha but Alonso Quijano" (984). His niece, he says, is Antonia Quijana (986).

This is obviously not the simple presentation of a list of alternatives, but is, as I believe further examples of the same process will demonstrate, part of a calculated campaign to keep the reader unsure and off balance, and is only fully exploited in Part II, with the ingenious deception involved in the inclusion of Part I within Part II, which will be discussed in Chapter 4. The two examples which follow illustrate the basic pattern, of which the confusion surrounding Don Quixote's real name is but one variant:

(1) The cause of Don Quixote's fatal illness: "Whether it was owing to melancholy occasioned by the defeat he had suffered, or was, simply, the will of Heaven which had so ordained it, he was taken with a fever . . ." *but*: "it was the doctor's opinion that melancholy and depression were putting an end to his patient's life" (983).

(2) The truth of the Cave of Montesinos episode: "As for this [adventure] of the cave, I see no way in which I can accept it as true, as it is so far beyond the bounds of reason," although "it is impossible for me to believe

19

that Don Quixote lied, since he is the truest gentleman and noblest knight of his age . . ." and "in so brief a space of time as that he could not have fabricated such a farrago of nonsense." *But*: "[*it is considered certain*] that at the time of his death [*they say*] he retracted what he had said, confessing that he had invented the incident . . ." (*665-66).

This last example is the most fully realized of the type. The author carefully expounds both sides of the case in doubt, then explicitly calls upon the reader to judge: "You, wise reader, may decide for yourself; for I cannot, nor am I obliged, to do any more" (666). "A deliberate mystification," says Edward Riley, one of the most careful readers of Cervantes. "Cervantes strews contradictory clues about, hedges the incident around with talk, and finally leaves the reader to judge for himself."[9] But does he? As before, when the reader feels that he is in possession of all the relevant considerations to make his own judgment on the issue of Don Quixote's credibility, the decision is immediately snatched back, *after* the reader has been advised to judge for himself: "[It is considered certain] that at the time of his death [they say] he retracted what he had said." Thus, though the resolution of the problem is not really left to the reader, not at the time nor on the terms that Cid Hamete has said it would be, neither is it accomplished by the author, who dissolves it in third-hand hearsay evidence. This confusion is absolutely essential as preparation for the tremendous enigma of Chapter XLI, when Don Quixote whispers in Sancho's ear: " 'Sancho,' he said, 'if you want us to believe what you saw in Heaven, then you must believe me when I tell you what I saw in the Cave of Montesinos. I need say no more' " (778).

The authorial uncertainty mentioned above regarding the relationship between Don Quixote and Dulcinea ("as the story goes"; "it is generally believed") is not without consequences, too, for it is precisely on this point that we need the author's help. Don Quixote gives two mutually contradictory versions:

9. *Cervantes's Theory of the Novel* (Oxford, 1962), p. 187.

In the course of the dozen years that I have loved her . . . I can truthfully swear that I have not seen her four times (204).

Have I not told you any number of times that I have never in all the days of my life laid eyes upon the peerless Dulcinea . . . but am enamored of her only by hearsay, as she is famous far and wide for her beauty and her wit? (563).

Sancho, to whom both of these comments are addressed, is in the same position as the reader, and offers essentially the same response to the second version as in the "basin-helmet" dilemma: "I would have you know that it was also by hearsay that I saw her and brought her answer to you" (563).

What is the effect of all this mystification on the reader? It seems to be twofold. First of all, the reader emerges from each of these cases slightly disoriented, and tends to reserve judgment in cases of doubt. In addition, the conviction grows that the author is just as helpless as the reader ("I cannot . . . do any more"), and therefore that the evidence for judging characters and situations must be gleaned from the presentation of these characters and situations themselves, rather than from authorial commentary, which is in fact the case in this novel. The irony is, however, that the disorientation of the reader produced by this technique has consistently been epitomized in the "basin-helmet" episode, "the classic example of the ambiguity of reality in *Don Quixote*,"[10] the effect of which is, or should be, really quite the opposite. The famous phrase which has become the basis of perspectivism and relativity in the novel is Don Quixote's: "This that appears to you as a barber's basin is for me Mambrino's helmet, and something else again to another person" (200). The truth is, however, that there is no one else in the world of the novel to whom the basin appears to be "something else again," nor is

10. Julián Marías, in his prologue to Denys A. Gonthier, *El drama psicológico del "Quijote"* (Madrid, 1962), p. 10; see also Jean Cassou, "An Introduction to Cervantes," in *Cervantes Across the Centuries*, p. 8.

there anyone but Don Quixote to whom it appears to be a helmet. The author explains Don Quixote's self-deception before the helmet is even won, and every reader and all other characters assent, though some of the latter may agree with Don Quixote in jest: "The truth concerning that helmet and the horse and horseman that Don Quixote had sighted was this . . . a brass basin . . . an ass . . . [a] barber" (158). Few issues are clearer in the novel, and the problem arises only when *statements* in *Don Quixote* about perspectivism are taken as evidence to support the intuitive appreciation of subtle narrative technique actually applied at other points. Perhaps this is one of the bases for the extraordinary disparity of critical opinion on the nature of reality in *Don Quixote*.

Américo Castro's position in 1925 was as follows: "If in Cervantes there is a general preoccupation, prior to all others, it is that of the nature of reality."[11] He modified it significantly in 1947: "Years ago I attempted to interpret *Don Quixote* with excessively Occidental norms, and I believed that Cervantes was interested on occasion in determining the nature of the reality that lies behind the fluctuation of appearance. But the problem of logical truth or error does not preoccupy the author; it is rather a question of showing that reality is always an aspect of the experience of the person who is living it."[12]

Despite this modification, his original position is still common in literary manuals and has been sustained by critics. Mark Van Doren, for example, said in 1958 that "the great, central question of the book [is] : What is reality?"[13]

In diametrical opposition are statements such as these, by Alexander Parker: "Reality [in *Don Quixote*] is not ambig-

11. *El pensamiento de Cervantes* (Madrid, 1925), p. 79, quoted in English translation in Richard Predmore, *The World of "Don Quixote,"* p. 53.
12. *Hacia Cervantes*, 3rd ed. (Madrid, 1967), p. 384.
13. *Don Quixote's Profession* (New York, 1958), p. 41. Cf. Manuel Durán, *La ambigüedad en el "Quijote"* (Xalapa, 1960), who finds that Cervantes creates "a feeling of ambiguity and uncertainty with respect to objective reality" (p. 128).

uous; the world is rational in and of itself";[14] by Erich Auer-
bach: "The whole book is a comedy in which well-founded
reality holds madness up to ridicule";[15] and, finally, by Richard
L. Predmore: "If it were Cervantes' intention that the reader
consider reality problematical, would he not have to conceal a
bit his own confident attitude toward it?"[16] As Predmore
makes abundantly clear, Cervantes shows that although
reality is often deceptive, and that any number of intellectual
and emotional impediments, as well as sensory inadequacies,
may prevent its accurate perception by a given subject, the
phenomenal world in which the characters live and move is
rational and consistent. The violation in Part II of this consistent and rational presentation of reality and its effect upon
the reader will be discussed in Chapter 4.

NOTHING BUT THE TRUTH

While many readers will take the obfuscations described in
the preceding pages as evidence of impaired omniscience on
the part of the author, the more perceptive are apt to count
them against authorial reliability, for they are signs of what
Sheldon Sacks has called a "split commentator," alternately
serious and ironic.[17] While it is true, as Wayne Booth has
observed, that "mystery" in the first reading of any novel is
replaced by "irony" in a second,[18] the absurdity of some of the
instances cited above is signal enough for the careful reader
at the first reading. The fictional Cervantes of the first eight
chapters is clearly a split commentator, and is perceived as
such by the reader very early in the novel, the distinction

14. "El concepto de la verdad en *Don Quijote*," *Actas de la Asamblea
Cervantina de la Lengua Española* (Madrid, 1948), p. 304.
15. *Mimesis. The Representation of Reality in Western Literature*,
trans. Willard R. Trask (Princeton, 1953), p. 347.
16. *The World of "Don Quixote,"* p. 56. Predmore is here quoting his
own position of 1953, but his modifications of 1958, in *El mundo
del "Quixote"* which he translated in 1967 ("I still believe this to be the
truth, but not the whole truth"), relate only to the difficulties of accurate perception and do not seem to limit the basic affirmation.
17. *Fiction and the Shape of Belief*, pp. 70 ff.
18. *The Rhetoric of Fiction*, pp. 255-56.

between serious evaluation and ironic commentary being heavily reflected in the choice of adjectives:

> The poor fellow used to lie awake nights (26)
>
> the weirdest, most laughable appearance (34)
>
> Such was the manner in which the valorous knight righted this particular wrong (44). ("Valorous" at this point and in these circumstances—the episode of Andrés —is heavily ironic.)
>
> the decency and decorum that are fitting in so heroic an account (581).

One of the striking features of *Don Quixote* is the scarcity of authorial commentary. The reader is *told* almost nothing about Don Quixote's character, and even such laconic statements as "In every respect [he] was the courteous and obliging gentleman" (251) are very rare, as are judgments such as this: "Who would not have laughed at hearing the nonsense the two of them talked, master and man?" (317). Both the fictional Cervantes of the first eight chapters and Cid Hamete Benengeli function almost exclusively as straight narrators, alternately presenting reality and Don Quixote's distortion of it. Commentary by Cid Hamete is as scarce as that of Cervantes, but in contrast to the split commentary of the latter, Cid Hamete is almost exclusively serious. The following examples illustrate the serious commentary:

> Let him bear it and hold his peace who is rash enough to attempt more than his strength will warrant (401).
>
> Here, Cid Hamete remarks, it is his personal opinion that the jesters were as crazy as their victims and that the duke and duchess were not two fingers' breadth removed from being fools when they went to so much trouble to make sport of the foolish (964).
>
> Don Quixote and Sancho then returned to their beasts and the life of beasts that they led (703).

The kind of ironic commentary one finds in Chapters I-VIII is absent from Cid Hamete's manuscript, and only in an occasional hyperbolic outburst does one find a note of irony:

> O great-souled Don Quixote de la Mancha, thou whose courage is beyond all praise, mirror wherein all the valiant of the world may behold themselves . . . (615).

> O perpetual discoverer of the antipodes, great taper of the world, eye of the heavens, sweet shaker of the water-coolers . . . 'tis thee whom I beseech to favor and enlighten my darkened intellect that I may be able to give an absolutely exact account of the government of the great Sancho Panza (797-98).

Given the lack of authorial commentary, the reader is left to form his judgments and adopt his ethical perspective toward the characters and events in the novel on the basis of the self-revelation of the characters, primarily in dialogue, and on the manner of presentation and the juxtaposition of events. The question of reliability, then, is essentially limited to the issue of authorial dependability in recounting events.

The fictional Cervantes is accepted by the reader as a trustworthy source for the activities of Don Quixote. He is dependent upon other sources, but maintains the illusion of objectivity toward them. The limitations on the reader's wholehearted acceptance of the author's account are three: (1) the deliberate mystification concerning Don Quixote's real name, (2) the ironic commentary, and (3) the ridiculous chronological contradictions reflected in the following information:

> In a village of La Mancha . . . there lived *not so long ago* one of those gentlemen (25).

> I reflected that inasmuch as among the knight's books had been found such modern works as *The Disenchantments of Jealousy* [1586] and *The Nymphs and Shepherds of Henares* [1587], his story likewise must be modern (70).

> A lead box . . . had been found in the crumbling foundation of a very old hermitage that was being rebuilt. In this box were discovered certain writings on parchment . . . which had much to say of [the feats of Don Quixote] (*460).

None of these limitations, however, is sufficient to dissuade the reader from accepting Cervantes' account as essentially accurate.[19]

The question of Cid Hamete's reliability is a somewhat different matter. First, doubts are cast upon his trustworthiness within the novel itself. These doubts are first expressed by Cervantes' fictional self: "If there is any objection to be raised against the veracity of the present [story], it can be only that the author was an Arab, and that nation is known for its lying propensities; . . . for whenever he might and should deploy the resources of his pen in praise of so worthy a knight, the author appears to take pains to pass over the matter in silence" (73). Don Quixote expresses similar reservations when he learns of the publication of Part I: "He was a bit put out at the thought that the author was a Moor, if the appellation 'Cid' was to be taken as an indication, and from the Moors you could never hope for any word of truth, seeing that they are all of them cheats, forgers, and schemers" (526). Cid Hamete himself fears he may not be believed in the matter of Sancho's enchantment of Dulcinea and, finally, doubt is once expressed as to the authenticity of the manuscript attributed to him: "As he comes to set down this fifth chapter of our history, the translator desires to make it plain that he looks upon it as apocryphal" (538).

These doubts raised within the book, however, are belied by the obvious accuracy and omniscience of Part I, as revealed in Part II. "No serious discrepancies emerge between [Don Quixote's and Sancho's] literary reputations [Part I] and their current selves in Part II."[20] Confidence is further reinforced by the contrast repeatedly drawn between Cid Hamete's "true" account and the false version by Avellaneda. The reader, not unaffected by the vindication of Cid Hamete's re-

19. It does not seem to me that the consequences of the chronological disparity are usually nearly so serious to the reader as they were to Gilbert Highet, *The Anatomy of Satire* (Princeton, 1962), pp. 116-19, who asks: "Did Quixote live in the year 1600 or the year 1300?" Don Quixote is clearly a near-contemporary of Cervantes.

20. Edward C. Riley, "Who's Who in *Don Quixote*? Or an Approach to the Problem of Identity," *Modern Language Notes*, 81 (March, 1966), 128.

liability within the novel itself, has few other reasons to accept the account less than wholeheartedly. Only twice is the reader misled, and both cases involve the introduction of minor characters. The first instance occurs with the arrival of the Distressed Duenna at the duke's palace: "It must be on account of those three points [of her skirt] that she was known as the Countess Trifaldi, as one might say: the Countess of the Three Skirts, an opinion that is supported by Benengeli, who asserts that the lady's right name was the Countess Lobuna and that she was so called on account of the many wolves in her country" (756). Countess Trifaldi is of course, as Cid Hamete himself will later reveal, "a major-domo of the duke's" (789).

The second deception occurs during the governorship of Sancho, when the farmer who is presented as making "a very favorable impression; for it could be seen from a thousand leagues away that he was a worthy man and a good soul" (813) turns out to be a "rogue [who] knew how to play his part very well" (815).

The reservations upon authorial reliability, then, both in the case of the fictional Cervantes and in that of Cid Hamete, are negligible, especially considering the great number of deceptive and confusing situations which are credibly clarified by the authors throughout the course of the novel. The reader perceives the account as accurate, and acceptable as a basis for a valid ethical perspective toward the characters and events. Cid Hamete's account is sufficiently complete, omniscient in important respects (with the single exception of the truth or falsity of the Cave of Montesinos episode), and almost entirely reliable, and his commentary, though infrequent, is consistently serious and rarely misleading. Cervantes has made the Moor's perspective his own by not challenging it at any important point in the transmission. Finally, as Riley indicates, one must observe that Cid Hamete and the fictional Cervantes do in fact merge in the reader's mind, and that the identity of purpose which they share—ridicule of the novels of chivalry—is a main factor in this fusion, together with other correspondences which he points out, such as "In a village of La Mancha the name of which I have no desire to recall . . ." (Cervantes, 25) and "whose birthplace Cid Hamete was unwilling to designate exactly" (987).[21] Beyond this, it would seem that the fundamental unity between the two authors lies in the mutual attitude of "affectionate reprobation" toward Don Quixote which the infrequent commentary reveals.[22]

21. *Cervantes's Theory of the Novel*, p. 209.

22. "Cervantes, writing as a champion of average reality, means us to respond to Don Quixote with affectionate reprobation . . ." according to Oscar Mandel, "The Function of the Norm in *Don Quixote*," p. 163.

2. CONTEXTUAL DISCLOSURE

It is in the treatment of character and situation rather than in character and situation *per se* that we get our initial clues as to how we are to evaluate them.

Sheldon Sacks, *Fiction and the Shape of Belief*, p. 95.

In order, Sancho, that you may see the good that there is in knight-errantry and how speedily those who follow the profession, no matter what the nature of their service may be, come to be honored and esteemed in the eyes of the world, I would have you here in the company of these good folk seat yourself at my side, that you may be even as I who am your master and natural lord, and eat from my plate and drink from where I drink; for of knight-errantry one may say the same as of love: that it makes all things equal" (80).

Most readers of *Don Quixote* will remember the knight's magnanimous invitation to Sancho during their stay with the goatherds. Friedrich Schürr, for example, quotes it as an example of "the most attractive feature of his character . . . his profound humanity and goodness,"[1] and Harry Levin seconds Melville's "enthusiasm for the knight's invitation to the squire," remarking: "Equality and love—the two themes blend in the meal with the goatherds that evokes Don Quixote's vision of the Golden Age."[2] Perhaps fewer readers remember Don Quixote's reaction when Sancho declines the offer: " 'But for all that,' said Don Quixote, 'you must sit down; for whosoever humbleth himself, him God will exalt.' And, laying hold of his squire's arm, *he compelled him to take a seat beside him*" (81).

This is an example of the kind of contextual signal for the evaluation of Don Quixote with which this chapter is con-

1. "Cervantes y el romanticismo," p. 52.
2. *"Don Quixote* and *Moby Dick,"* in *Cervantes Across the Centuries,* p. 221.

31

cerned, and which we are now prepared to examine, fore-warned that the author of the first eight chapters is a split commentator, and realizing that Cid Hamete is a generally omniscient, essentially reliable narrator whose commentary is almost always straightforward and serious. The goal of this examination must be the identification of those subtle devices of disclosure which affect our reactions to the protagonist and which produce the intriguing ambivalence and sharp differences of opinion among the critics.

First of all, there is significance in the specific attraction the chivalry novels hold for Don Quixote. Cervantes' explicit statements throughout the novel as to its purpose—ridicule of the novels of chivalry—force a careful examination, as do the widely varying critical opinions about what exactly it was that Don Quixote intended to revive: "Of all those [books of chivalry] that he thus devoured none pleased him so well as the ones that had been composed by the famous Feliciano de Silva, *whose lucid prose style* and involved conceits were as precious to him as pearls; especially when he came to read those tales of love and amorous challenges that are to be met with in many places, such a passage as the following, for example: 'The reason of the unreason that afflicts my reason, in such a manner weakens my reason that I with reason lament me of your comeliness'. . . . The poor fellow used to lie awake nights in an effort to disentangle the meaning and make sense out of passages such as these" (26). The first attraction of the chivalry novels for Don Quixote, then, was the *style,* and his favorite author was Feliciano de Silva, whose "diabolic and involved conceits" (53) led the curate, "a [great] friend" of Cervantes (*57), to burn his books. It is the altisonant and archaic language of the novels of chivalry that Don Quixote himself employs in his first sally, "stringing together absurdities, all of a kind that his books had taught him, imitating insofar as he was able the language of their authors" (31).

What were the actions of the chivalric heroes which attracted Don Quixote? "*Above all* [the knights-errant] he cherished an admiration for Rinaldo of Montalbán, *especially* as he beheld him sallying forth from his castle to rob all those that crossed his path" (27). These superlatives make it clear that at this point Don Quixote's desire to "right every manner of wrong" (27) is only a means to his ultimate goal, which is to win "eternal glory" (27). "As a reward for his valor and the might of his arm, the poor fellow could already see himself crowned Emperor of Trebizond at the very least" (27-28). He looks forward to the time when his "famous exploits shall be published, exploits worthy of being engraved in bronze, sculptured in marble, and depicted in paintings for the benefit of posterity" (31). At this point Don Quixote does not perceive even the most blatant ridicule by other characters. The innkeeper who later is to knight him offers an extended parody in Chapter III of chivalric activity in the account of his youth, when he had, as he says, "done many wrongs, cheated many widows, ruined many maidens, and swindled not a few minors" (37), and Don Quixote seems not to notice.

It is difficult to escape the conclusion that the initial reaction to the protagonist as he sallies forth from the inn is that he is a ridiculous and vain figure, with whom one does not identify and at whom one is prepared to laugh. Given this initial relationship between reader and protagonist, the most significant point for scrutiny lies in Don Quixote's defeats. What is it in each case that allows the reader to laugh at Don Quixote in defeat, and, more significantly, what prevents laughter and provokes sympathy, identification, or admiration?

Don Quixote, PART I

Don Quixote's first adventure after leaving the inn is the episode of Andrés and Juan Haldudo, in which Andrés "went away weeping, and his master stood laughing at him" (44). Cervantes, in the role of ironic commentator, intrudes immediately with the following: "Such was the manner in which the *valorous* knight righted this particular wrong. *Don Quixote was quite content with the way everything had turned out . . . and he was very well satisfied with himself* as he

33

jogged along in the direction of his native village"(44).
"Valorous" is ironic, as has been indicated above, and is in fact
not an authorial contribution, but a mocking repetition of Don
Quixote's own words a few moments before: "In case you
would like to know who it is that is giving you this command
in order that you may feel the more obliged to comply with it,
I may tell you that I am the *valorous* Don Quixote de la
Mancha" (43). But "quite content with the way everything
had turned out," and "very well satisfied with himself" (44),
is straightforward commentary, and counts heavily against
Don Quixote with the reader, who is consequently well prepared to enjoy his defeat at the hands of the Toledan merchants: "Don Quixote went rolling over the plain for some
little distance, and when he tried to get to his feet, found that
he was unable to do so. . . . One of the muleteers . . . took the
knight's lance and broke it into bits, and then with [one of the
pieces] proceeded to belabor him so mercilessly that in spite
of his armor [he] milled him like a hopper of wheat" (*46).
The balance of justice in the world of the novel has been restored, and Don Quixote has paid, not for an error in perception or judgment but for his foolish vanity.

In Chapter VII, the reader sees that Don Quixote has not
learned from his initial unfortunate experience, and he rises
again to dangerous presumption in conversation with his
niece: "Before they shear me, I will have plucked and stripped
the beards of any who dare to touch the tip of a single hair of
mine" (60), and with Sancho: "It well may be that within a
week I shall win some kingdom with others dependent upon it,
and it will be the easiest thing in the world to crown you king
of one of them" (62). Immediately after this exchange, Don
Quixote attacks the windmills and is thrown, "rolling over the
plain, very much battered indeed" (63).

Signs of the protagonist's vanity and presumption are less
extreme in the episode of the windmills, and there is no in-
justice as in the case of Andrés, so even though the fall is less
severe, the reader is not prepared to accept another defeat
without considerable further preparation. The next adventure

is Don Quixote's first real victory, over the valorous Biscayan, and the success in that encounter and his reaction to it bode ill for the knight, for this is what prepares the reader to accept and laugh at his next defeat. This defeat, at the hands of the Yanguesans, is separated by the episode of Marcela and Grisóstomo from Don Quixote's expression of arrogance upon defeating the Biscayan: "Have you ever seen a more valorous knight than I on all the known face of the earth? Have you ever read in the histories of any other who had more mettle in the attack, more perseverance in sustaining it, more dexterity in wounding his enemy, or more skill in overthrowing him?" (76). Nevertheless, the peculiarly inaccurate subtitle to Chapter X reveals the pride-fall link in the author's mind: ["Of what else happened to Don Quixote with the Biscayan and of the danger in which he found himself with a mob of Yanguesans"] (*75), and is perhaps indicative of the order of narration in a more primitive version, before the interpolation of the pastoral sequence.[3] At any rate, Cervantes drives the connection home sharply immediately after the defeat, when Don Quixote tells Sancho: "You already know by a thousand proofs and experiences the valor of this, my strong right arm" (110), to which the narrator adds: "For the poor gentleman was still feeling puffed up as a result of his victory over the valiant Biscayan" (110). Sancho also makes the connection: "Who would have thought that those mighty slashes your Grace gave that poor knight-errant would be followed posthaste by such a tempest of blows as they let fall upon our shoulders?" (111). It is in this context that one must consider the famous "I am worth a hundred" of Don Quixote upon charging the Yanguesans (109).

Once again Don Quixote has been soundly beaten, and he

3. Geoffrey Stagg argues persuasively for precisely this juxtaposition of Chapters X and XV in a primitive version, in "Revision in *Don Quixote*, Part I," *Hispanic Studies in Honor of L. González Llubera*, ed. Frank Pierce (Oxford, 1959), pp. 347-66. Putnam's translation of the title of Chapter X follows an emendation which appears in many later Spanish editions, ignoring the original because of its obvious inaccuracy. The emendation: "Of the pleasing conversation that took place between Don Quixote and Sancho Panza, his squire."

retires to Juan Palomeque's inn to recover. The next encounter is to be a serious one, the battle with the muleteer over Maritornes, and therefore the preparation is extensive. It begins with the initial address to the innkeeper's wife: "Believe me, beautiful lady, you well may call yourself fortunate for having given a lodging in this your castle to my person" (116). The second stage is the knight's erotic fantasy concerning the innkeeper's daughter: "He fancied that . . . the daughter of the lord (innkeeper) who dwelt there, having been *won over by his gentle bearing, had fallen in love with him* and had promised him that she would come that night, without her parents' knowledge, to lie beside him for a while" (118). To culminate the process, Don Quixote "held out his arms as if to receive the beautiful maiden. . . . Seizing her firmly by the wrists, he drew her to him. . . . Forcing her to sit down upon the bed, he began fingering her nightgown. . . . Clasping her tightly, he went on to speak to her in a low and amorous tone of voice," protesting too much his inability to satisfy her desires, although "the girl was doing her best to free herself and Don Quixote was trying to hold her" (118-19). Preparation for a comic denouement is now accomplished, and the knight is beaten severely by the muleteer.

The equilibrium of justice is again restored in the novel. Don Quixote's pertinacity, together with our confidence by this point in the novel that nothing seriously damaging, physically or psychologically, will happen to him (a presupposition of Part II which turns out to be mistaken), predispose us for the next peccadillo, and when the knight says, in Chapter XVIII: "This . . . is the day when you shall see the boon that fate has in store for me; this, I repeat, is the day when, as well as on any other, shall be displayed the valor of my good right arm. On this day I shall perform deeds that will be written down in the book of fame for all the centuries to come" (131), one knows another defeat must be forthcoming; this time it is the adventure of the two flocks of sheep.

The victory over the white-shirted figures escorting the dead body follows upon this defeat. It is interesting to compare the boast quoted above, which prepared the previous defeat, with Don Quixote's much milder statement before this encounter: "There can be no doubt, Sancho . . . that this is going to be a very great and perilous adventure in which it will be necessary for me to display all my strength and valor" (139). Not enough, especially given the mystery surrounding the encounter, "which, if it was not a real adventure, certainly had all the earmarks of one" (139), to cause the reader to expect or desire the knight's defeat.

The adventure of the fulling mills, which follows this victory, is extremely significant for an understanding of the ethical perspective from which the author has indicated that the reader should view the activities of Don Quixote. Here, Sancho, at the close of the episode, illustrates the proper reader reaction, and Don Quixote clearly demonstrates just where he is missing the mark in his attitudes and behavior. He approaches the adventure with a typically vain and grandiloquent oration, and when the fulling mills are seen to be just that, and not giants, Sancho cannot keep from laughing. Don Quixote laughs, too, at the deception, but he becomes furious when Sancho begins to mock his previous vanity by recalling his speech: "You may know that I was born, by Heaven's will, in this our age of iron, to revive what is known as the Golden Age. I am he for whom are reserved the perils, the great exploits, the valiant deeds" (146, 154). This is one of two times in the novel when he actually strikes Sancho. "But turn these six hammers into six giants and beard me with them one by one, or with all of them together, and if I do not cause them all to turn up their toes, then you may make as much sport of me as you like" (155). Don Quixote has missed the point of Sancho's parody. It is not an attack upon his valor, or even upon his feeble strength. It is the deflation of his vain and pretentious oratory. Don Quixote can laugh at the disparity between illusion, "six giants," and reality, "six fulling hammers," which for many critics is the tragic element of the novel. What he cannot abide is the revelation of his vanity and presumption. This episode contrasts vividly with the episodes in Part II presented as successfully accomplished simply by virtue of the valor of the attempt (Clavileño, the episode of the lions). The difference between them is not in the activity, the nobility, or the bravery of Don Quixote, but in the author's presentation, controlled by the effect which he wishes to produce upon the relationship between reader and protagonist.

Don Quixote's next adventure is the victory of the helmet of Mambrino, and it is followed by the episode of the galley slaves, a mixed affair, with victory over the guards annulled by the stoning of Don Quixote and Sancho by the freed prisoners. The real conclusion of this episode, in terms of Don Quixote's humiliation, does not occur until much later, after the introduction of Dorotea and Cardenio and, again, only after the reader is brought to the point of expecting the hero to suffer. Upon meeting him in the Sierra Morena, Dorotea, in the guise of the princess Micomicona, has heaped praises on Don Quixote, who replies as follows: "That will be enough! Let me hear no more words of praise! For I am opposed to any kind of adulation and even though this be no fawning, such talk for all of that offends my chaste ears" (255). Don Quixote's reference to his "chaste ears" has certainly tipped the balance, and the reader is greatly amused when, after the curate describes the man who had freed the galley slaves as "out of his mind, or . . . as great a villain as they" (255), Sancho promptly reveals that "the one who performed that deed was my master" (256).

One of the best examples of the rise and subsequent fall to humiliation which has become the pattern of Don Quixote's existence as knight-errant is to be found in the episode which next concerns us, and it involves at the same time a link with the first example of the process—the boy Andrés. On meeting Andrés again, Don Quixote takes him by the hand, leads him before the group of travelers, and delivers the following speech:

"In order that your Worships may see how important it is to have knights-errant in the world to right the wrongs and injuries done by the insolent and evil beings who inhabit it, you may know that some while ago, as I was passing through a wood, I heard certain pitiful cries . . . and there I found, bound to an oak tree, this lad who now stands before you. . . . I compelled the peasant to release the boy and made him promise to take him home and pay him every real of what he owed him, and perfumed into the bargain. Is not that all true, Andrés, my son? *Did you not note how imperiously I commanded him to do that and with what humility he promised to carry out all my orders and instructions?* Speak up and tell these ladies and gentlemen, clearly and in a straightforward manner, just what happened; for I would have them see and be convinced that I was right when I said that it is very useful to have knights-errant going up and down the highroads" (271-72).

The humiliation which follows is total:

"He not only did not pay me," said the boy, "but the moment your Grace had left the wood and we were alone, he tied me to that same tree again and gave me so many fresh lashes that I was like St. Bartholomew when they had done flaying him."

. . . .

"For the love of God, Sir Knight-errant, if ever again you meet me . . . do not aid or succor me but let me bear it, for no misfortune could be so great as that which comes of being helped by you. May God curse you and all the knights-errant that were ever born into this world!" (272-73).

Don Quixote recedes into the background after this humiliation for much of the next hundred pages of the novel. The "Story of the One Who Was Too Curious for His Own Good," the solution of the problems of Luscinda and Cardenio, and Dorotea and Fernando, the captive's story, and the reunion of the judge and his brother occupy the reader's attention during this interval, and Don Quixote's participation is limited to the battle with the wineskins (involving neither victory nor defeat, in terms of this discussion), and the speech on Arms and Letters, which, while not important in the pride-fall pattern here being discussed, is an important step in the deepening of the reader-protagonist relationship, and as such will be discussed later.

When Don Quixote reappears at the center of the stage in Chapter XLIII, it is to prepare the way for another humiliation, for the reader must again be disposed to laugh at the hero's discomfiture. As he guards the inn, Don Quixote hears the innkeeper's daughter calling him, and again "it occurred to his insane imagination that, as on a previous occasion, the daughter of the lord of this castle, *overcome with love of him,* was seeking to make a conquest" (392). She asks for his hand, and Don Quixote replies: "Lady, take this hand, or better, this avenger of the world's evildoers. . . . I extend it to thee, not that thou shouldst kiss it, but that thou mayest study the contexture of the sinews, the network of the muscles, the breadth and spaciousness of the veins, from which thou canst deduce how great must be the might of the arm that supports such a hand" (393).

This passage cries out for deflation, not simply of Don Quixote's pride in the nonexistent strength of his arm, but also of the very verbosity of his remarks. As Castro has pointed out in another connection, "ultra-expressiveness, the accumulation of words, usually gives evidence of a double or oblique meaning (irony or defensive caution)."[4]

The girls tie his wrist to the door, and Don Quixote finds himself immobilized, "and then, at last, morning found him so despairing and bewildered that he brayed like a bull" (394).

The last two defeats of Part I—the encounter with the shepherd who tells the story of Leandra, and the battle with the penitents—are not preceded by the kind of preparation present in previous cases. This lack of preparation may well be responsible for the slight note of ambivalence which characterizes one's feelings toward both the curate and the canon at the end of Part I. These characters have been presented very sympathetically throughout. The curate is a perceptive literary critic, friend of Cervantes, charitable toward Don Quixote, "so good a Christian and so honest a man that he

4. *Hacia Cervantes,* p. 370*n.*

would not for anything in the world utter an untruth" (54), one who "generally speaks with the voice of the author's strictest critical conscience."[5] The canon is an intelligent critic, man of letters, and gentle remonstrator of Don Quixote. It may be that the reader's misgivings about their reactions to Don Quixote's fight with the goatherd ("the canon and the curate were laughing fit to burst" [454]) and to Sancho's lament over the fallen knight after the encounter with the penitents ("weeping and wailing in the most lugubrious and, at the same time, the most laughable fashion" [456]) are due not to a change in the sense of the comic since the seventeenth century, as some critics have suggested, but to a lack of the kind of preparation at work before. The reader has laughed at worse beatings more than once, but Don Quixote did not seem to *deserve* these as he has others.

One has come to marvel at his ingenuity in adapting reality to his preconceptions, to believe, by the force of his persistence, in the sincerity of his intentions, however vain, and to admire his commitment and his eloquence. The speech on Arms and Letters, much superior in originality and in appropriateness to the situation than the discourse of the Golden Age, awakens pity, not only in the other characters, but in the reader, "at seeing a man, who to all appearances was perfectly sensible and able to discuss any other topic quite rationally, so hopelessly lost whenever the subject of chivalry came up, for that was his dark, pitch-black obsession" (343). It is increasingly true as the novel progresses that the reader will not laugh at Don Quixote in defeat unless specifically directed to do so by the author's rhetorical signals. Nevertheless, Don Quixote remains, at the close of Part I, a vain and meddling man with whom one does not identify strongly, at best occasionally pathetic, never tragic, almost always the object of readers' and other characters' laughter.[6]

---

5. Riley, *Cervantes's Theory of the Novel*, p. 29.

6. In search of an impartial listing of Don Quixote's defeats to corroborate my interpretation here, I find in Predmore's book (*The World of "Don Quixote,"* p. 20) that "six [adventures] are clearly failures (merchants, windmills, flocks of sheep, dead body, fulling

Don Quixote, PART II

Radical differences separate Part I from Part II, as to the reader's attitude toward Don Quixote. Only a few of these may be subsumed under Madariaga's "Sanchification" of Don Quixote, important as that process is to the problem at hand.[7] To Don Quixote's increasing cognizance of reality must be added the loss of control of events ("I can do no more" [703]), in which the central elements are the knight's powerlessness to effect the disenchantment of Dulcinea and the increase in deception practiced upon him, the much wider display of intelligence, eloquence, and discretion, the increasing element of self-doubt, the rise to new heights of audacity, and the shift of emphasis in Don Quixote's own mind from the reliance on the strength of his arm to a growing insistence upon the strength of his spirit. Important, too, is a marked difference in the moral stature of his opponents, for, as Oscar Mandel has observed, "the [ethical] status of a protagonist is invariably a factor of the status of his opponents."[8] Sansón Carrasco, the agent of Don Quixote's return in Part II, does not measure up to the standard of the curate, who fulfilled

---

mills, penitents); and three more are essentially failures even though for a time they may wear some semblance of success (Andrés, galley slaves, wineskins)." Of these, I have not dealt with the adventure of the dead body, since it seems to me to be clearly a victory, nor with that of the wineskins, which involves neither victory nor defeat in terms of this discussion. I cannot see any reason for not considering the beating by the Yanguesans, the muleteer-Maritornes fracas, the tying up of Don Quixote by Maritornes, and the drubbing by the shepherd as clear defeats, though Predmore could of course exclude them for his purposes as not being *chivalric* defeats.

7. Salvador de Madariaga, *"Don Quixote." An Introductory Essay in Psychology* (London, 1961), pp. 146-56.

8. "The Function of the Norm in *Don Quixote,*" p. 162. The fascinating diversity of critical opinion which motivated the writing of the present study forces the realization that the reverse of Mandel's observation is also true: the ethical status of the protagonist's opponents can be seen as a factor of *his* status. E.g., Mandel himself, in the article cited here: "Almost all secondary and minor characters represent the acceptable 'norm,' especially the Man in Green, an ethical focus for the entire novel" (p. 160), *vs.* Américo Castro: "Don Diego is not there to embody an exemplary type of enlightened gentleman, of Christian gentleman . . . he is situated on the prosaic side of life" (*Cervantes y los casticismos españoles* [Madrid, 1966], pp. 138-39).

that function in Part I, and the ecclesiastic at the duke's palace is in direct contrast to the gentle, compassionate canon of Part I. A similar contrast may be seen, too, between Dorotea and Altisidora in Parts I and II, respectively.

The increasing cognizance of reality, Don Quixote's loss of control over events, and the increase in number and complexity of deceptions practiced upon him are too well known to require further comment, but it seems worthwhile to allude to the many displays of eloquence, erudition, and wit in Part II, which contrast sharply with the single example of the speech on Arms and Letters from Part I. In the second part, Don Quixote discourses upon the true knight (546, 618), lineage (546-48), fame (558-59), the upbringing of children (608), poetry (609), marriage (630-31), the model wife (649-50), the just war (690-91), liberty (882), and gratitude (889), in addition to the much quoted advice to Sancho on the latter's assumption of the governorship of Barataria.

The element of self-doubt becomes increasingly poignant as Part II progresses. The "I can do no more" (703) of a particular encounter in Chapter XXIX becomes the "up to now, I do not know what I have won with all the hardships I have endured" (884) of Chapter LVIII, and the process culminates after Don Quixote's defeat in Barcelona, when he says, in Chapter LXVI: "Each man is the architect of his own fortune. I was the architect of mine, but I did not observe the necessary prudence, and as a result my presumptuousness has brought me to a sorry end" (943). This is the companion piece to Don Quixote's original affirmation in Chapter IV, Part I: "Every one is the son of his works" (43), and it is surely to this self-knowledge that Sancho refers as they arrive home for the last time: "Open your arms and receive also your other son, Don Quixote, who returns vanquished by the arm of another but a victor over himself" (978).

As has been noted in Chapter 2 above, there is almost no direct commentary by the author in Part II about Don Quixote's character, beyond a belated recognition of his increasing cognizance of reality: "Ever since he had been overcome in combat he had talked more rationally on all subjects" (972), and such brief, infrequent general indications as "being very courteous and fond of pleasing everyone" (605). Don Quixote himself, however, formulates significant statements about his character with which the reader cannot but agree: "I thank Heaven that it has endowed me with a tender and compassionate heart, always inclined to do good to all and evil to none" (677), and: "My intention is always a worthy one: that of doing good to all and harm to none" (717). Sancho, in turn, corroborates: "I can assure you there is nothing of the rogue about him; he is as open and aboveboard as a wine pitcher and would not harm anyone but does good to all. There is no malice in his make-up, and a child could make him believe it was night at midday. For that very reason I love him with all my heart and cannot bring myself to leave him, no matter how many foolish things he does" (588). These are all indications of the "Alonso Quijano the Good" behind Don Quixote, who is only to emerge in the last chapter of Part II.

The shift in emphasis from physical to spiritual strength begins very early in Part II, when the knight refers obliquely to himself in Chapter I as a knight-errant, who, "if not so [fierce] as the knights of old, will not be inferior to them in the matter of courage" (*514). He returns to the theme in Chapter XVII: "The enchanters may take my luck away, but to deprive me of my [spirit] and courage is an impossibility" (*617). At times it is reflected in the weight of adjectives in a departure from the usual balanced pairs: "The strength that lies in my arm and in the undaunted resolution of my stout heart" (753), and at other times it may seem little more than the formal reticence of courtly discourse: "Here are my arm and my courage which, though weak and insufficient, are wholly at your service" (757-58); "owing to the limited means at my disposal, I do hereby offer you what lies within my power" (889). The process is nevertheless in operation throughout, and it is inexorable.

This, then, must be the background for the examination of

Don Quixote's defeats in Part II: Increased sympathy for a protagonist who increasingly reveals himself to be an intelligent, well-intentioned, self-doubting man, the victim of his fellow man as well as of his own presumption.

Don Quixote's increased perceptiveness becomes immediately obvious. It has been pointed out that at the beginning of Part I, Don Quixote was oblivious of the innkeeper's parody. In Chapter I of Part II he is immediately aware of the point of the barber's story about the madman of Seville. The discourse which follows on the difference between knights-errant and knights at court is only the beginning of a series of eloquent speeches, as has been indicated above.

It is also significant that over two hundred pages of Part II pass without Don Quixote having suffered a single defeat. It is not until Chapter XXIX that he is thrown from the enchanted boat, and the preparation is so slight ("I am Don Quixote de la Mancha . . . for whom it is reserved, by order of the highest heavens, to bring this adventure to a fortunate conclusion!" [702]), that the reader rebels against Cid Hamete's comment at the close of the chapter: "Don Quixote and Sancho then returned to their beasts and the life of beasts that they led" (703). Casalduero's explanation to the effect that to return to "the life of beasts," in the light of Sancho's comments on page 573, indicates a return to sadness does not, even if correct, mitigate the reader's irritation at the apparent harshness.[9]

Don Quixote's humiliating fall from his horse in his first encounter with the duke and duchess takes one by surprise, but the recovery is so superb that it is sufficient to restore equilibrium in the novel: "Whatever might have happened to me, valorous prince . . . could not possibly have been evil, even though I had fallen all the way to the depths of the bottomless pit; for the great honor of meeting you would have raised me up and delivered me. . . . But in whatever state I may be, fallen or erect, on foot or on horseback, I shall always be at your service and that of my lady the

9. Joaquín Casalduero, *Sentido y forma del "Quijote,"* p. 253.

duchess, your worthy consort, beauty's deserving queen and sovereign princess of courtesy" (707). The fall is reduced to insignificance.

Don Quixote's next humiliation is more serious, and hence requires preparation if the reader is to accept it in a comic vein. It follows a great deal of eloquence and wit on Don Quixote's part, including his brilliant rebuttal of the ecclesiastic and the advice to Sancho, and is, in addition, the first really serious reverse suffered by the knight in Part II. The preparation for the encounter with the cats recalls the adventure with Maritornes in Part I. Hearing a harp being played beneath his window, "he at once fancied that one of the duchess's waiting women must be enamored of him" (794). It is Altisidora who is below, however, and she is acting the love-struck damsel, so one must hear more from Don Quixote before one can accept the scratching by the cats: "Oh, why must I be so unfortunate a knight that no damsel who looks upon me can help falling in love with me! Why must it be the misfortune of the peerless Dulcinea del Toboso not to be left in peace to enjoy my incomparable fidelity! What would you of her, O queens! Empresses, why do you persecute her! Why do you pursue her, O maids of fourteen and fifteen years of age! Leave, oh, leave the wretched one to rejoice in her triumph and to glory in the lot that Love has bestowed upon her. . ." (796-97).

The reader knows that this kind of presumptuousness will not go unpunished, and of course it does not, but it is a measure of the reader's increased attachment to Don Quixote, and of the intensity of his suffering ("Don Quixote's face was perforated like a sieve and his nose was not in very good shape. . . . It did cost him five days in bed" [807-8]), that Altisidora cannot go ultimately unpunished, though the final retribution is thirty-four chapters away (966). The reader gains some satisfaction in Chapter XLVIII on finding out that "her breath is so bad that one cannot bear to be near her for a moment" (822).

The pinching which Don Quixote and Doña Rodríguez suffer

at the hands of Altisidora and the duchess is perhaps the last episode in which Cervantes permits the reader to laugh unreservedly at Don Quixote's expense. The preparation is slight, but the defeat is not serious, and can be accepted in a comic vein.

> Who knows . . . but that the devil, who is subtle and cunning, may be trying to deceive me now with a duenna, which is something he has not been able to accomplish with empresses, queens, marchionesses, or countesses? (818)
>
> I do ask you if I am safe from being attacked and raped (819).

This is certainly preparation enough, with this variant of the pattern so well established.

Following the stay at the duke's castle, with the end of the governorship of Sancho and the victory over Tosilos in defense of Doña Rodríguez' daughter, the reader enters what can be considered the crucial section of the novel, in terms of the equilibrium of justice. It lies between the two episodes in which Don Quixote is rather gratuitously trampled, first by bulls in Chapter LVIII and later by pigs in Chapter LXVIII, and in the same spot, near the feigned Arcadia. These ten chapters contain seven defeats or humiliations, including the climactic and definitive defeat at the hands of the Knight of the White Moon, and they show the protagonist at his lowest ebb, though paradoxically at his finest hour. All of the preparation—the established pattern of pride and fall, the accumulation of affection and admiration that is the product of bits and pieces of eloquence, wit, charity, nobility, valor, generosity, patience, and fortitude—is brought to bear at this point, and the sensitive reader suffers with a man at whom he has repeatedly laughed for some eight hundred pages.

The introduction of this process has already been quoted in part. It comes at the conclusion of the episode of the images: "Up to now, I do not know what I have won with all the hardships I have endured. However, if my lady Dulcinea were but free of those that she is suffering, it may be

47

that my fortunes would improve, and with a sounder mind I should be able to tread a better path than the one I follow at present" (884). Then, the trampling by the bulls: "As a result the wild bulls and the tame leading-oxen . . . passed over Don Quixote and over Sancho, Rocinante, and the gray as well, knocking them all down and sending them rolling" (891). Ten pages later Don Quixote suffers the humiliation of a defeat at the hands of Sancho, when, losing all patience at Sancho's lack of progress in the disenchantment of Dulcinea, he attempts to force the issue by administering himself the necessary lashes to his squire: "Sancho leaped to his feet and charged at him. Grappling with him man to man, he tripped him up and brought him down flat on his back, and then placing his right knee on the knight's chest, he grasped his master's hands and held them in such a way that the poor fellow could neither stir nor breathe" (900). The shock to the reader, aware of Sancho's total ultimate dependence upon his master, is considerable, and this dependence, together with Don Quixote's complete lack of rancor, is immediately brought out by Cervantes: "Sancho then rose and walked away. . . . Just as he was about to lean back against another tree, he felt something touching his head, and, raising his hands, he found that it was a pair of feet with shoes and stockings on them. Trembling with fright, he ran over to another tree, and the same thing happened, whereupon he began shouting at the top of his voice, calling upon Don Quixote to come and help him. The knight did so . . ." (901). Eschewing commentary, and even dialogue, Cervantes has with one stroke revealed the nobility of soul of his protagonist: "The knight did so." Juxtaposition of events in context is consistently the principal method by which Cervantes directs the reader's sympathies and ethical judgments.

Interspersed among the next five defeats and humiliations suffered by Don Quixote are occasional echoes of the former presumption, no longer sufficient to balance the falls: "I am Don Quixote de la Mancha, with whose exploits the whole world is filled" (902); "puffed up and self-satisfied" (914) in

Don Antonio Moreno's house, where he was treated as a knight-errant. Trampled by bulls, beaten by Sancho, thrown from his horse during the triumphal entry into Barcelona, insulted in the street by the Castilian during what Unamuno has called the *via crucis* of the hero, the nadir of the knight's social existence is reached at the *sarao* given by Don Antonio Moreno:

> He was a sight to see: long, lean, lank, and yellow-looking, clad in his tight-fitting suit, awkward, and, above all, not very light on his feet. The frolicsome ladies made furtive love to him and he, likewise by stealth, rejected their advances; but, finding himself hard pressed by these attentions, he finally raised his voice and cried out, "*Fugite, partes adversae!* Leave me in peace, unwelcome temptations! Away with your passion, ladies; for she who is queen of my heart, the peerless Dulcinea del Toboso, will consent to none other assailing it and laying it low!"
>
> Saying this, he sat down in the middle of the ballroom floor, battered and broken from his exertions . . . (918).

If Don Quixote has given more emphasis to spiritual than to physical strength in Part II, it is also true that the defeats are more of the spirit, for these ladies "wore him out, not only in body but in spirit as well" (918).

The stage is now set for the definitive defeat of Don Quixote by the Knight of the White Moon. Sansón Carrasco is merciless: "I come to contend with you and try the might of my arm, with the purpose of having you acknowledge and confess that my lady, *whoever she may be,* is beyond comparison more beautiful than your own Dulcinea del Toboso. . . . Let me have your answer at once, for *today is all the time I have* for the dispatching of this business" (935). Don Quixote's response is impeccable, without a note of undue pride. After unhorsing him, Sansón places his lance at the knight's visor: "You are vanquished, O knight! Nay, more, you are dead unless you make confession in accordance with the conditions governing our encounter" (937).

Don Quixote's response in defeat to his opponent's demand is his finest moment: "Dulcinea del Toboso is the most beauti-

ful woman in the world and I the most unhappy knight upon
the face of this earth. It is not right that my weakness
should serve to defraud the truth. Drive home your lance,
O knight, and take my life since you already have deprived me
of my honor" (937).

The final humiliation, when Don Quixote and Sancho are
trampled by pigs, closes the sequence, and though Don
Quixote is not yet cured of his insanity, he has vanquished
his pride, which is much more important. In these circum-
stances, the reader relishes the authorial commentary on the
duke and duchess: "Here, Cid Hamete remarks, it is his per-
sonal opinion that the jesters were as crazy as their victims
and that the duke and duchess were not two fingers' breadth
removed from being fools when they went to so much trouble
to make sport of the foolish" (964). Revenge is also sweet in
the case of Altisidora, and her frustration at the lack of
success in seducing Don Quixote is beautifully underplayed.
There is no authorial comment, only a sudden explosion of
anger, from which she quickly recovers, but during which she
drops the pose of love-struck damsel: "By the living God, Don
Codfish! Soul of a brass mortar, date-stone harder and more
obdurate than an ignorant rustic when you ask him to do you a
favor and he has made up his mind to the contrary! Just let
me throw myself on you and I'll scratch your eyes out! Do you
perhaps think, Don Vanquished, Don Cudgeled, that it was
for you I died?" (966).

One moves, then, from laughter and ridicule to sympathy
and admiration, and Don Quixote's opponents and deceivers,
who in Part I—the curate, the canon, Dorotea—represented
in large measure the reader, have come in Part II to be our
opponents—Sansón Carrasco, the duke and duchess, the ecclesiastic, Altisidora.

In investigating the victories and defeats of Don Quixote,
Predmore finds no consistent attempt to "reward good intentions [or] an accurate reading of reality," nor can he say
that "the punishments [are] always graduated to fit the of-
fense." He is therefore forced to concede that he "found it

impossible to adjust them fully to any discoverable moral order."[10] As this chapter has attempted to demonstrate, the difference between adventures is not essentially in the justice, sanity, nobility, or bravery of Don Quixote, but in the author's presentation, which depends upon a fundamental "moral order" shared by Cervantes and his readers. The examination of Cervantes' maintenance of the balance of justice in the novel through the equilibrium of pride and punishment, and the alteration in Part II of this balance by a series of "undeserved" defeats and humiliations, corroborates the perceptive comments of Alexander Parker: "The essence of it is that his boastful vanity corrupts his ideal and weakens and destroys it in practice. . . . In order that the innate goodness of Don Quixote become the measure of his actions, his ideal must be purified of all egotism. He must renounce his arrogant ambition, he must humble himself to the point where he recognizes the reality of things and of himself."[11]

10. *The World of "Don Quixote,"* pp. 20-27.
11. "El concepto de la verdad en el *Quijote*," pp. 297-300.

3. STYLISTIC DISCLOSURE

The history of literature, in its broadest sense, appears to be a continual breach of levels of style (high style being profaned, low style elevated) or a history of metaphorical transference (sacred attributes being secularized, and vice-versa).

Geoffrey Hartman, "Structuralism: The Anglo-American Adventure," in *Structuralism*, Yale French Studies (New Haven, 1966), p. 168.

The walls of the inn where Sancho and Don Quixote spent the night in Chapter LXXI of Part II were adorned with leather hangings depicting the abduction of Helen of Troy and the separation of Aeneas and Dido. "Helen did not appear very reluctant about going, for she was laughing slyly and roguishly, but the beauteous Dido was shedding tears the size of walnuts . . . [and] signaling with half a sheet to the fugitive" (972). This passage suggests the central question which lies behind the radical divergence of critical opinion in the interpretation of Cervantes' novel. The "crude hand" of the painter of these classical scenes had unconsciously ridiculed his noble subjects. In *Don Quixote*, has Cervantes (consciously, of course) hidden a truly heroic figure behind a presentation which only makes him *seem* ridiculous, as the painter had done, or has he given us a protagonist who *is* indeed ridiculous? The conclusion of Chapter 2 has been that it is Cervantes' presentation of Don Quixote as *being* ridiculous, not as simply seeming ridiculous, which determines the reader's ethical orientation. It is not a mask behind which Cervantes hides his admiration for a misunderstood hero.

A proper analogy does exist, however, between the painter and Don Quixote in their ridiculous imitations of heroic subjects. Though Don Quixote has chosen the noblest aspects of the novels of chivalry as objects of imitation, his vanity and presumption make comedy of what would otherwise inevitably become pathetic or tragic. An examination of the contribution of stylistic contrast to the ethical orientation of the reader supports Américo Castro's assertion that "the sound of the style in *Don Quixote* depends upon the key which the author selects, upon the *intent.* . . . *Don Quixote* is not a sample-book of styles . . . there is something here *significant* in terms of poetic *intent.*"[1] This poetic intent includes the determination of the ethical stance of the reader vis-à-vis the protagonist, and is indeed reflected in language and style as well as in the nature and disposition of the action and commentary.

•   •   •

First of all, the archaic language of the novels of chivalry is clearly a negative element. It is to be counted against Don Quixote, and thus serves to prepare the comic denouement of certain episodes or to obstruct the pathetic or tragic reaction. The negative function of chivalric archaism is established at the very outset of the novel, as reflected in the passage quoted in the previous chapter where the curate, undisputed spokesman for Cervantes on literary matters, joins the fictional Cervantes in condemning the "stiffness and dryness of . . . style" (53) and "absurdities" (31) of the novels.

The pseudo-archaic flavor of the novels of chivalry is captured by Cervantes in three essential characteristics: (1) retention of initial *f* in Spanish words from the Latin which by 1605 had evolved to *h* (*fermosa>hermosa*; *fizo>hizo*) ; (2) retention of certain archaic verb forms in the second person plural (*habedes>habéis*) ; and (3) an archaic and somewhat specialized vocabulary (*ca, desaguisado, membrar, pro*).[2] Unfortunately, these characteristics are very imperfectly communicated in translation, and no translation reflects with any precision the distribution of their use in *Don Quixote.* An examination of the phenomenon in the Spanish original proves very interesting. First, one notices that the use of chivalric archaism is greatly diminished in Part II. This is obvious to the Spanish reader, and is usually associated with Don Quixote's returning sanity.[3] More interesting for our purposes here is the fact that chivalric archaism is used by Don Quixote in connection with every one of the eleven defeats in

1. *Hacia Cervantes*, pp. 271-72.
2. The first two of these characteristics are given as elements of Cervantes' chivalric archaism by Julio Cejador y Frauca, in *La lengua de Cervantes*, I (Madrid, 1905), 57, 129-30.
3. See, e.g., Madariaga, *"Don Quixote,"* p. 183.

Part I discussed in Chapter 2, and is not used by him in connection with any of the defeats in Part II, with the exception of the humiliating fall on meeting the duke and duchess; however, he does employ archaic language on at least five other occasions in Part II, and Sancho, Sansón Carrasco, the duke, Doña Rodríguez, and the author all use it at times. Furthermore, chivalric archaism is not used at many points where it might have been expected if it functions as an identifying tag for the chivalric (e.g., the Arms and Letters speech, pages 338-43), or for Don Quixote's insanity (e.g., pages 333-34). Don Quixote does not use it after Part II, Chapter XXXII.

This investigation indicates that chivalric archaism in *Don Quixote* serves a more important purpose in fostering an expectation of—or helping to justify—comic deflation. The adventure of the fulling mills, again, is a revealing episode. When Sancho mocks Don Quixote's pompous speech ("Sancho, my friend, you may know that I was born by Heaven's will, in this our age of iron, to revive what is known as the Golden Age. I am he for whom are reserved the perils, the great exploits, the valiant deeds . . ." [154]), he *adds* an archaism ("deeds" = "*fechos*") which the knight had not injected into the original ("*hechos*"). The escalation in archaism is a subtle part of Sancho's joke, and an added irritation to his master.

•　•　•

The most pervasive and significant elements of the stylistic contribution to the ethical orientation of the reader, however, are to be found in the various forms of antithesis, so basic to Cervantes' literary technique. As Riley has observed, "the use of antithesis is fundamental not only to his style, but to the whole technique of construction in *Don Quijote*."[4] It will have been obvious, from the contextual disclosure of proper ethical perspective examined in Chapter 2, that the most common preparation for a response of laughter to Don Quixote's encounters is the protagonist's proud hyperbole which fairly demands deflation:

> You already know by a thousand proofs and experiences the valor of this, my strong right arm (110).

4. *Cervantes's Theory of the Novel*, p. 31.

> I am he for whom are reserved the perils, the great exploits, the valiant deeds (146).
>
> I am opposed to any kind of adulation, and . . . such talk . . . offends my chaste ears (255).
>
> "Who knows," he said to himself, "but that the devil, who is subtle and cunning, may be trying to deceive me now with a duenna, which is something he has not been able to accomplish with empresses, queens, marchionesses, or countesses?" (818).

An analogous effect is achieved by the author more directly, through a deliberate inequity, approaching antithesis, between style and content in certain descriptive passages. There is almost no description of nature in *Don Quixote*. Flaubert alludes to this fact in a famous remark: "Comme on voit ces routes d'Espagne qui ne sont nulle part décrites!"[5] It is not surprising, then, that the six rather highly stylized descriptions of dawn in the novel have received some special comment. The commentators have seen that the significance of these descriptions lies in their relationship to the immediate context, just as we have seen the contextual relationship between adventures as basic in the disclosure of ethical perspective. The dawn descriptions follow:

> (1) No sooner had the rubicund Apollo spread over the face of the broad and spacious earth the gilded filaments of his beauteous locks, and no sooner had the little singing birds of painted plumage greeted with their sweet and mellifluous harmony the coming of the Dawn, who, leaving the soft couch of her jealous spouse, now showed herself to mortals at all the doors and balconies of the horizon that bounds La Mancha—no sooner had this happened than the famous knight, Don Quixote de la Mancha, forsaking his own downy bed and mounting his famous steed, Rocinante, fared forth and began riding over the ancient and famous Campo de Montiel (31).
>
> (2) At that moment gay-colored birds of all sorts began warbling in the trees and with their merry and varied songs appeared to be greeting and welcoming the fresh-dawning day, which already at the gates and on the

5. *Correspondence*, II, 305, quoted by José Ortega y Gasset in *Meditaciones del "Quijote"* (Madrid, 1956), p. 56.

balconies of the east was revealing its beautiful face as it shook out from its hair an infinite number of liquid pearls. Bathed in this gentle moisture, the grass seemed to shed a pearly spray, the willows distilled a savory manna, the fountains laughed, the brooks murmured, the woods were glad, and the meadows put on their finest raiment. The first thing that Sancho Panza beheld, as soon as it was light enough to tell one object from another, was the Squire of the Wood's nose, which was so big as to cast into the shade all the rest of his body (595).

(3) Scarcely had the fair Aurora given the glowing Phoebus an opportunity to dry the liquid pearls upon her golden locks with the warmth of his rays when Don Quixote, shaking off all sloth from his limbs, rose to his feet and called to his squire Sancho, who was still snoring (635).

(4) With this, the merry-smiling dawn hastened her coming, the little flowers in the fields lifted their heads, and the liquid crystal of the brooks, murmuring over their white and gray pebbles, went to pay tribute to the waiting rivers. The earth was joyous, the sky unclouded, the air limpid, the light serene, and each of these things in itself and all of them together showed that the day which was treading on the skirts of morning was to be bright and clear (747-48).

(5) O perpetual discoverer of the antipodes, great taper of the world, eye of the heavens, sweet shaker of the water-coolers, Thymbraeus here, Phoebus there, archer in one place, in another a physician, father of poetry, inventor of music, thou who dost ever rise and, though appearing to do so, dost never set! 'Tis thee, O Sun, by whose aid man doth beget man, 'tis thee whom I beseech to favor and enlighten my darkened intellect that I may be able to give an absolutely exact account of the government of the great Sancho Panza (797-98).

(6) It was not long before the fair Aurora began to show herself on the balconies of the east, bringing joy to the grass and flowers [instead of to the ear] (*911).

Clemencín, in his 1833-39 edition of *Don Quixote*, commented as follows upon the description from Part II, Chapter

XX (635) : "The climax of the passage contrasts comically with its beginning; the snores of Sancho with the approach of Aurora."[6] Edward Riley concurs as he specifies the source of the comic effect in the first of the series: "Cervantes achieves his comic effect less through the description of dawn itself than by relating the activities of the deities with those of Don Quixote and Rocinante."[7] Finally, Angel Rosenblat has characterized the whole series as follows: "In all the dawn descriptions the altisonant note is brought down by the comic situation or by an abrupt note of realism: the nose of the Squire of the Woods, Sancho's snores, day treading on the skirts of morning."[8]

In order to appraise the effect upon the ethical perspective of the reader, it is necessary to go beyond the recognition of the comic to an assessment of the type of comic contrast and the object of humor—the butt of the joke.

To begin with, it would seem that the six examples are evenly divided between two basic types of dawn description, epic and lyric, which Riley identifies, quoting the examples given by Cervantes' contemporary, Alonso López Pinciano, in his *Philosophia antigua poética* (1596).[9] The second, fourth, and sixth examples fit the type of lyric description illustrated by López Pinciano. As Rosenblat points out, the humor in the second example results from the beautiful-grotesque contrast, and in the fourth from the internal inadequacy within the description itself ("the day which was treading on the skirts of morning"). Although Riley comments that the sixth example "seems to be conventional and serious," it is like the fourth, in that the humor results internally from the *non sequitur* "instead of to the ear."[10]

6. *El ingenioso hidalgo Don Quijote de la Mancha* (Madrid: Castilla, 1948), p. 1625, note 2.
7. "El alba bella que las perlas cría," *Bulletin of Hispanic Studies*, XXXIII (1956), 132.
8. "La lengua de Cervantes," in *Cervantes* (Caracas, 1949), pp. 53-54.
9. "El alba bella," pp. 126-27. Riley does not divide the examples from *Don Quixote* into epic and lyric.
10. *Ibid.*, p. 136n. Clemencín, again, has noticed the anomaly, but seems confused by it: "What connection does the dawn have with the ear?" (p. 1885, note 3).

None of these burlesque lyric dawn descriptions, then, are achieved at the expense of Don Quixote or any other character. The other three instances, all of the mock-epic variety, seem to deflate the characters involved to some degree in each case, by the implicit contrast between the epic style and the less-than-epic protagonists. The first example is quite obviously funny at Don Quixote's expense, especially since he is its author, as he imagines how the book of his exploits will begin. The humor of the remark with which Cervantes follows this passage: "And this was the truth, for he was indeed riding over that stretch of plain," arises from the incongruity of the reader's receiving verification of the insignificant and acceptable point in the passage and no comment at all on the outrageous hyperbole.

In the second mock-epic description (635) the possibility arises that, as in the first example, Don Quixote will be the lower term of the contrast: "Don Quixote, shaking off all sloth from his limbs. . . ." But as both Clemencín and Rosenblat have testified, Sancho's snores, being the lower point, receive the weight of the contrast and become the focus of the humor. The last example, a mock-epic invocation, is clearly aimed at Sancho and his government, and parallels the first example, with Sancho taking the role which Don Quixote played in the earlier instance. This passage has its counterpart at the conclusion of the governorship, when Sancho explains his departure:

> I was not born to be a governor.
>
> .   .   .   .
>
> These jokes won't do a second time. . . . In this stable I leave behind me the ant's wings that lifted me in the air so that the swifts and other birds might eat me: let's come back to earth and walk with our feet once more, and if they're not shod in pinked Cordovan leather, they'll not lack coarse hempen sandals (858-59).

The counterpart to the first dawn description, aimed at Don Quixote, is not dissimilar:

> I realize how foolish I was.
>
> .   .   .   .

61

Leave all jesting aside and bring me a confessor for my sins and a notary to draw up my will. In such straits as these a man cannot trifle with his soul.

.   .   .   .

I was mad and now I am sane; I was Don Quixote de la Mancha, and now I am, as I have said, Alonso Quijano the Good (984-86).

The parallel between the presumption and repentance of Sancho and that of Don Quixote is further reinforced by the similarity between the passages which introduce, respectively, the end of Sancho's governorship and Don Quixote's death:

To imagine that things in this life are always to remain as they are is to indulge in an idle dream. It would appear, rather, that everything moves in a circle, that is to say, around and around: spring follows summer, summer the harvest season, harvest autumn, autumn winter, and winter spring; and thus does time continue to turn like a never-ceasing wheel. Human life alone hastens onward to its end, swifter than time's self and without hope of renewal, unless it be in that other life that has no bounds. So sayeth Cid Hamete, the Mohammedan philosopher; for many who have lacked the light of faith, being guided solely by the illumination that nature affords them, have yet attained to a comprehension of the swiftness and instability of this present existence and the eternal duration of the one we hope for. Our author, however, is here thinking of the speed with which Sancho's government was overthrown and brought to a close, and, so to speak, sent up in smoke and shadow (855-56).

The subject is no longer "the government of the *great* Sancho Panza," and, though there is humor in the passage ("that is to say, around and around"; "the Mohammedan philosopher"), it is not directed at Sancho, and the seriousness of the analogy (death: governorship) and the level of style contrast with the mock-epic invocation just examined. The passage compares very well with the preparation for the death of Don Quixote:

Inasmuch as nothing that is human is eternal but is ever declining from its beginning to its close, this being especially true of the lives of men, and since Don Quixote was not endowed by Heaven with the privilege of staying the downward course of things, his own end came when he was least expecting it (983).

There is a sense, then, in which the brief governorship of Sancho—mock-heroic preparation, essentially comic, though surprisingly laudable exercise of the new profession, change to a serious tone in preparation for the denouement, confession, and repentance—parallels in its principal outlines the genesis, practice, and renunciation by Don Quixote of his chivalric mission. The parallel is actualized by careful modulation of stylistic level and tone as much as by any other technique.

Of the dawn descriptions, as we have seen, only the first deflates Don Quixote, and nothing in this realm of stylistic disclosure attests so strongly to the change in his stature in Part II as the comparison of these six pretentious dawn descriptions with the morning of Don Quixote's defeat by the Knight of the White Moon: "And then, *one morning,* as Don Quixote went for a ride along the beach, clad in full armor— for, as he was fond of saying, that was his only ornament, his only rest the fight, and, accordingly, he was never without it for a moment—he saw approaching him a horseman . . ." (935).

· · ·

Another type of contribution to the deflation of Don Quixote is the near antithetical inadequacy of words spoken by one or another of the characters at certain points in the novel, and often presented as inadvertent slips. The process involves the displacement of an expected element, or of one of an expected class of elements, by another, unexpected element, absurd in its inadequacy or inappropriateness. At the close of the adventure of the fulling mills, Sancho remarks that: "[*only the*] *sound of fulling hammers* can disturb and agitate the heart of so valiant a knightly adventurer as is your Grace" (*156). "The sound of fulling hammers" has displaced something terrible in the reader's expectation.

63

Dorotea, as the Princess Micomicona, recognizes Don Quixote in the Sierra Morena, "for the signs of his face are in accord with the high repute which this knight enjoys not only in Spain but *throughout La Mancha*" (259). "Throughout La Mancha" has displaced "throughout the world," though, ironically enough, La Mancha is more accurate.

Don Quixote comments on his artistic potential, in conversation with his niece prior to the third sally: "I can tell you one thing, niece, that if my mind were not so wholly occupied with thoughts of chivalry, there is nothing that I could not do, no trinket that I could not turn out with my own hands, *especially birdcages and toothpicks*" (548). "Birdcages and toothpicks" have displaced some ingenious work of art on the level of the chivalric activities which now occupy the knight.

It is interesting to consider this last example in the light of Gerald Brenan's comments on the realistic touches in Don Quixote's account of his adventures in the Cave of Montesinos: "These affect us not merely by their sudden reduction of high romance to the crudest reality: their comedy is finer than that, for it consists in their being indications of a fundamental dryness and prosaicness in the mind of this man who has set himself up against the prosaic scheme of things."[11]

A slightly different mechanism operates in the case of Sancho's slip of the tongue in the soliloquy on the search for Dulcinea, whom he seeks, "[for] the famous knight, Don Quixote de la Mancha, who rights wrongs and *gives food to the thirsty and drink to the hungry*" (567).

Sancho has simply interchanged "thirsty" and "hungry," but the ironic appropriateness of the result recalls the conclusion of some of Don Quixote's earlier adventures, e.g., the second meeting with Andrés, whom he had tried to help: "For the love of God, Sir Knight-errant, if ever again you meet me, even though they are hacking me to bits, do not aid or succor me but let me bear it, for no misfortune could be so great as that which comes of being helped by you. May God curse you and all the knights-errant that were ever born into this

11. *The Literature of the Spanish People* (New York, 1957), p. 189.

world!" (273). Or Alfonso López' response to Don Quixote's assertion of his duty to "go through the world righting wrongs and redressing injuries": "I do not know what you mean by righting wrongs, seeing that you found me quite all right and left me very wrong indeed, with a broken leg which will not be right again as long as I live; and if you have redressed any injury in my case, it has been done in such a way as to leave me injured forever" (142).

A second example of this device, though less directly appropriate, occurs in Sancho's lament over the fallen Don Quixote in the closing pages of Part I: "Humble with the proud, haughty with the humble" (457).

The best testimony of the derogatory effect of these slips is the fact that they must be deleted when the passage is cited in support of the exaltation of Don Quixote, as in the following quotation, which appears in conjunction with a discussion of Don Quixote's self-affirmation, in which he is compared to Saint Paul: "O flower of chivalry! . . . O honor of your line, honor and glory of all La Mancha and of all the world! . . . O master more generous than all the Alexanders! . . . *Humble with the proud* . . . brave in facing dangers, long-suffering under outrages, in love without reason, imitator of the good, scourge of the wicked, enemy of the mean—in a word, a knight-errant, which is all there is to say."[12] The ellipsis has turned a slip of the tongue into praise of Don Quixote's Christian virtue of humility.

All five of the above cases of comic displacement are directed against Don Quixote, and although only the first two are directly related to humiliations of the protagonist, all occur before the third sally, in Part II. The single additional example is applied to Dulcinea, and by Don Quixote himself: "I would swear that my Dulcinea del Toboso . . . is today [as intact as the mother who bore her]" (*210-11). This case is similar to Sancho's mistake with thirst and hunger, since

12. Quoted in the original Spanish, but with ellipsis as indicated throughout, by Denys Gonthier, *El drama psicológico del "Quijote"* (Madrid, 1962), p. 82. The italics are mine.

here, too, there has been a switch between two similar expressions. Don Quixote's reference to Dulcinea's virginity should have been "as her mother bore her," but he has used instead the even more common "as the mother *who* bore her" which, of course, means precisely the opposite. This expression counts against Don Quixote directly (the foolish mistake contrasts with his usually precise sense of language) and indirectly (we suspect the statement is true *as it stands* of Aldonza Lorenzo, after Sancho's description of her a few pages before—"there's nothing prudish about her; she's very friendly with everybody and always laughing and joking" [205],[13] as was Sancho's assertion above that Don Quixote "gives food to the thirsty and drink to the hungry"). Don Quixote and his faith in Dulcinea's purity have already been deflated in the context anyway, since Don Quixote has just expressed the conviction that Dulcinea has not gone the way of Angélica, who "had slept . . . more than two siestas with Medoro, a young Moor with curly locks," because Dulcinea "in all the days of her life has never seen a single Moor, as he is, in his native costume" (210-11). These examples of comic displacement are not particularly numerous—six in all —but it seems significant that in every case they are directed against Don Quixote.

Our examination of the contribution of language and style to the determination of proper ethical perspective reveals again that Cervantes both presents Don Quixote as being a fool, *and* makes a fool of him in the first part of the novel. The reader's changing judgment of the protagonist is abetted by the diminution and eventual disappearance of chivalric archaism, which was previously associated more closely with the knight's vanity and presumption than with chivalric context or insanity, by the avoidance of mock-epic deflation of Don Quixote, and by the elimination of the innuendos involved in the kind of comic displacement we have just witnessed.

13. The innuendo in the Spanish, *"no es nada melindrosa, porque tiene mucho de cortesana,"* is untranslatable, since it depends upon the "courtesan" connotation of *cortesana.*

4. LEVELS OF FICTION

This is a false awakening, being merely the next layer of your dream, as if you were rising up from stratum to stratum but never reaching the surface, never emerging into reality. . . . Yet who knows? Is this reality, *the* final reality or just a new deceptive dream?

Vladimir Nabokov, *King, Queen, Knave,* trans. Dmitri Nabokov (New York, 1968), pp. 20-21.

There is a vast amount of "acting" in Don Quixote, quite apart from the possibility suggested by Mark Van Doren that this is in fact Don Quixote's real profession—actor, and not knight-errant.[1] From the very first episodes of Part I, the characters often accept the roles assigned them by Don Quixote, beginning with the innkeeper who knighted him, and the second part abounds with elaborately staged productions designed to deceive and mock both Don Quixote and Sancho. The appearance of Merlin and his entourage with instructions for the disenchantment of Dulcinea, the governorship of Sancho, the puppet show of Maese Pedro, and the reception given to Don Quixote in Barcelona are a few examples. The roles assumed by the characters are at times given an ironic twist, as in the encounter in the Sierra Morena between Don Quixote and Dorotea, when the mad knight acts the part of a crazed lover in imitation of Amadís and Roland. Dorotea has taken the role of the Princess Micomicona in an effort to lure Don Quixote back home, and the result is a confrontation between a mad knight playing the part of a mad knight, and a damsel in distress playing a damsel in distress. These brief indications will suffice to recall the abundance of acting in the novel. It is necessary here to penetrate the book at the deepest level of fiction-within-fiction, and reconstruct the various layers from that point to the surface, as preparation for an examination of the peculiar interpenetration which develops between two of the levels.

The last and smallest in this series of Chinese boxes is to be found in the "Story of the One Who Was Too Curious for His

1. *Don Quixote's Profession.*

Own Good," from Part I of the novel. The story, apparently drawn in part from Ariosto's *Orlando Furioso*, Canto 43, has been left behind by a guest at the inn of Juan Palomeque, and is read by the curate to the assembled travelers. This "exemplary novel" is the story of Lotario and Anselmo, "the two friends," as they were known in Florence, where the action takes place, and of Anselmo's bride Camila. Anselmo begs Lotario to attempt to seduce Camila, as a test of her fidelity. Lotario reluctantly accepts, and the story runs its logical course to the tragedy which follows Anselmo's discovery that his friend and his bride are lovers.

The moment of interest here occurs when Anselmo, having pretended to leave his house, conceals himself to await the arrival of Lotario, who has told him in a fit of jealousy that Camila has indeed fallen. By the time of the meeting, Lotario has repented of the disclosure, and he and Camila, aware that Anselmo is watching, are prepared to offer him a convincing display of Camila's conjugal fidelity.

The principal actors in this little play, then, are Lotario and Camila, with Lotario acting the part of Camila's lover. At the next level, however—that of Anselmo, the spectator—Lotario is Anselmo's friend. Anselmo, and indeed the whole town, consider this to be the level of reality. The third level is that of the "real" Lotario, Camila's lover. Just as the mad Don Quixote decided to assume the role of mad knight in the Sierra Morena, so Lotario the lover has seen fit to superimpose the *role* of lover on his basic pose as Anselmo's friend. Of course, all of this is fiction for the characters at the fourth level, that of Don Quixote and the others at the inn. It is a short story, criticized by the curate for its lack of plausibility and praised for its style.

Perhaps the relationship among the various levels thus far will be clearer if it is put in terms of a more familiar use of the play within a play. In *Hamlet*, had Claudius himself played the part of the murderous king in the traveling players' production, the levels would correspond, and the reader of Shakespeare's play would stand at the same remove from the play within as Don Quixote and the others at the inn stand from the scene with which we began. This is the level of *Don Quixote,* Part I, which must be seen in the light of the next level as Don Quixote's life story, for Part I and Part II are *different* levels of fiction.

The relationship between Part I and Part II is analogous to that between the interpolated story with which we began and Part I. In Chapters III and IV of Part II, Part I is commented on and criticized, and in much greater detail than was the "Story of the One Who Was Too Curious for His Own Good" in Part I. It is even corrected, modified, and amplified by Don Quixote and Sancho. Part II is the level of the "real" Don Quixote. Of course, this, too, is fiction, and its immediate casing is the manuscript of Cid Hamete. Between Cervantes and Cid Hamete stands the Moor who translated the manuscript into Spanish, and finally the reader's source is, of course, Cervantes' version. We have now arrived at our level of reality, or fiction, as the case may be, and are in a position to see the profusion of layers which separates us from our starting point in the fictional depths of the novel.

It is obvious that the components of the outer shell which includes the versions of Cid Hamete, the translator, and Cervantes, are not levels in the same sense as the others. But they are more than the superficial layers of the novels of chivalry which they parody. The thirteenth-century *Caballero Cifar,* for example, is presented by its author as a Spanish version of a Latin translation of a Chaldean original, but none of these has any real existence within the work. Cid Hamete is a *character* in *Don Quixote,* who, as he says, would have given his best coat to witness the encounter between Don Quixote and Doña Rodríguez in the duke's palace. His account is repeatedly placed under suspicion because he is Moorish. The translator, too, as was indicated in Chapter 1, edits and enters the text to make comments, as in this excerpt from Part II: "As he comes to set down this fifth chapter of our history, the translator desires to make it plain that he looks upon it as apocryphal, since in it Sancho Panza speaks in a manner that does not appear to go with his limited intelligence and indulges in such subtle observations that it is quite impossible to conceive of his saying the things attributed to him. However, the translator in question did not wish to leave his task unfinished . . ." (538).

It should be pointed out also that the juxtaposition of levels is not necessarily consistent throughout. The level of Cid Hamete is, in a fundamental sense, equidistant from Part I and Part II, although *within Part II* the illusion of one further remove is created.

The primary effect of these devices is the enhancement of the illusion of reality, as has been pointed out by more than one critic in discussing isolated relationships within the series here presented. Predmore, for example, on the effect of the "Story of the One Who Was Too Curious for His Own Good": "Since everything in *Don Quixote* is really literature, this relationship [between literature and life] is an artistic illusion achieved by establishing two fictional levels so separated that the difference which separates them seems to the reader to be the difference between literature and life."[2] And further: "The story of the *Man Too Curious for His Own Good* contributes to the same illusion. . . . It establishes another fictional level, which we regard from the same point of view as the Priest and his listeners. One might say that for a time we sit down beside them and lend them some of our reality."[3] The principle is valid, although, as we have seen, not one but several other levels of fiction have been established.

Aubrey Bell, in his book on Cervantes, felt the same effect at another point in the series, the existence of Part I within Part II: "In the Second Part of *Don Quixote,* the Knight of the Lions is accompanied by his shadow, the Knight of the Sorrowful Countenance, now crystallized in the printed page of Part I, so that any doubts we may entertain concerning the reality of the shadow only make the living Don Quixote more real."[4]

2. *The World of "Don Quixote,"* pp. 2-3.   3. *Ibid.,* p. 10.
4. Aubrey F. G. Bell, *Cervantes* (Norman, Okla., 1947), p. 97.

As several critics have observed, it is *here,* in the relationship between the fifth and sixth levels, as they have just been presented, between Part I and Part II, that the most fertile interpenetration of levels lies. Luis Rosales dedicates more than sixty pages of his monumental *Cervantes y la libertad* to the investigation of the extremely complex implications of this relationship, and Américo Castro has considered his 1924 article on the subject, "Cervantes y Pirandello," important enough to re-edit for inclusion in a 1960 volume. The contribution of Castro, and of Rosales along lines suggested by Castro's original article, lies in the detailed analysis of the new dimension given to Don Quixote and Sancho in Part II, through the introduction of the historical account of their previous activities which Part I represents. The new situation begins to develop at the close of Chapter II of the second part, with Sancho's report to Don Quixote:

> "Bartolomé Carrasco's son came home last night. He has been studying at Salamanca and has just been made a bachelor. When I went to welcome him, he told me that the story of your Grace has already been put into a book called *The Ingenious Gentleman, Don Quixote de la Mancha.* And he says they mention me in it, under my own name, Sancho Panza, and the lady Dulcinea del Toboso as well, along with things that happened to us when we were alone together. I had to cross myself, for I could not help wondering how the one who wrote all those things down could have come to know about them."
>
> "I can assure you, Sancho," said Don Quixote, "that the author of our history must be some wise enchanter" (525).

At this point, as Castro points out, "the main characters of *Don Quixote* begin to show us the double personalities of real beings, who live and move to and fro, and of literary characters, at the mercy of the 'second' existence which a writer was pleased to concede to them."[5]

5. "Cervantes y Pirandello," in *Hacia Cervantes,* p. 480. This point is also taken up from another perspective by Casalduero: "We are [involved] in the theme of the play within a play . . . the union of the real figure and the artistic figure through humor." *Sentido y forma del "Quijote,"* pp. 219-24.

But the relationship between the "story" of Don Quixote and his "real" existence does not remain one of simple juxtaposition:

> Don Quixote remained in a thoughtful mood as he waited for the bachelor Carrasco, from whom he hoped to hear the news as to how he had been put into a book, as Sancho had said. . . . If it was true that such a history existed, being about a knight-errant, then it must be eloquent and lofty in tone, a splendid and distinguished piece of work and veracious in its details.
>
> This consoled him somewhat, although he was a bit put out at the thought that the author was a Moor, if the appellation "Cid" was to be taken as an indication, and from the Moors you could never hope for any word of truth, seeing that they are all of them cheats, forgers, and schemers. He feared lest his love should not have been treated with becoming modesty but rather in a way that would reflect upon the virtue of his lady Dulcinea del Toboso (526).

We are presented here, as Castro says, with "the character's fear of not being understood by the author."[6] The final step in this illusion of the emancipation of the character from the author's control is taken in Chapter LIX, when someone comments that the spurious Part II contains an account of Don Quixote's participation in the jousts of Saragossa, and the knight's reply is as follows: "I will not set foot in Saragossa but will let the world see how this new historian lies, by showing people that I am not the Don Quixote of whom he is speaking" (898). Thus the character, in Castro's words, "has rebelled against the author, and aspires to live his own life as he sees fit."[7]

Luis Rosales clarifies the significance of Cervantes' achievement by a comparison of the similar devices employed by Pirandello in *Six Characters in Search of an Author* and by Miguel de Unamuno in his novel *Niebla*. On Pirandello, he concludes: "One could say—and it is true—that they are not the ones who originate their own drama; rather, on the contrary,

6. Page 481.   7. Page 485.

they originate in it. They are not defined by their character; they are defined by the life situation in which they are dramatized. . . . What matters to Pirandello is the consciousness of the character *as character*."[8]

Unamuno, deeply influenced by Cervantes, as his *Life of Don Quixote and Sancho* reveals, succeeds in *Niebla* in advancing still further along the same lines, as Rosales convincingly demonstrates. Augusto Pérez, the principal character in the novel, decides to commit suicide, and consults with the author, who informs him that this would be impossible, since Pérez does not exist. Augusto Pérez, as Rosales says, "does not feel *fixed* to certain acts [as do the characters of Pirandello]. He thinks he can change them, although he may not do so. . . . Without ceasing to consider himself a fictional character, he does not identify his personality with his 'role.' "[9]

Don Quixote breaks through all of these restrictions and affirms his freedom over against the fixed, possibly inaccurate, representation of him in Part I.

We have seen, then, that the novel presents a complex series of different levels of fiction, and that the relationship between two of these levels (Part I and Part II) provides the vehicle for an unprecedented illusion of autonomy for Don Quixote, unequaled even by those who have employed similar devices in our own times.

But something else is happening with the appearance of Part I within Part II which bears directly upon the problem of the nature of reality in the world of *Don Quixote*. As we saw above in Chapter 1, Don Quixote coexists in the same world with Madame Bovary, Raskolnikov, and the rest of us. It is *our* world, however distinctively Don Quixote may interpret it. If there are enchanters at work in Don Quixote's world, surely their reality and *modus operandi* are those of Santa Claus in ours.

8. *Cervantes y la libertad. La libertad soñada* (Madrid, 1960), II, 205.
9. Pages 214-15.

This is true right up to the point in Part II that we have been discussing. Cervantes, or Cid Hamete, tells us that Don Quixote fought windmills, stole a barber's basin, and engaged in a number of other rather unconventional activities, all of them undertaken in *our* world, and governed by the same physical and psychological principles which define our activity. The enchanters work only through the mind of the knight, as they do in our world. For those who would take issue with this basic fact about the book, one can only recommend Predmore's book, which clearly separates the firm ground of reality in the novel from its very considerable liability to misinterpretation by the characters.

What Predmore, and, for that matter, Castro and Rosales, neglect to discuss is the conclusive manner in which that reality, the phenomenal world of *Don Quixote,* is totally unhinged precisely at the point which we have been examining, and that this results not from the creative activity of Don Quixote, but from a trick played by Cervantes on the reader. As we have seen above in Chapter 1, Cervantes is obviously a master at deliberate confusion. Who wrote Part I? Who wrote this partial biography of Don Quixote and Sancho, of which there are 12,000 copies in print already, according to Sansón Carrasco, who has just finished reading it? We may cite Don Quixote's answer to that question: "I can assure you, Sancho, that the author of our history must be some wise enchanter" (525). It is all very well for Don Quixote to say this. The idea that an omniscient Moor has written an account of his activities and private thoughts of not thirty days before, and that the account is already translated into Spanish and published all across western Europe is no strain on his credulity. It is consistent with his view of the nature of reality. The trouble is, of course, that this time he is right. There is no explanation for this state of affairs but enchantment. Enrique Moreno Báez has noticed this anomaly, "wholly fictitious, and so artfully interwoven with the rest of the narration that only when we analyze it do we realize its complete inverisimilitude," but he seems to see only the inverisimilitude of the rapid appearance in print and the fact that it was known, for example, to Roque Guinart, "who, because of the hazards of his profession, could not be up on the latest literary novelties."[10] Edward Riley seems to see most clearly the significance of what has happened: "The Knight invents an enchanter-chronicler and proceeds to believe in him. . . . He is miraculously realized in fact and presents proof of his existence through the publication of Part I. The implications of this are formidable. It is a vindication of all his beliefs, for it means that chivalresque enchanters do exist outside the Knight's fancy—a point which Cervantes wisely refrains from pursuing, however. . . . The existence of Cide Hamete is a joke—and such a successful one that the significance of his absurdity is almost invariably passed over. He offers the one instance of total inverisimilitude in the book, with the exception of Don Alvaro Tarfe, who is a comparably peculiar case."[11]

But Riley, having grasped the "formidable implications" of this situation, notes only that "by making a patently unbelievable character supposedly responsible for the story, Cervantes wraps his vivid simulacrum of historical reality safely in an envelope of fiction." The implications are more formidable yet, because more is at stake than the immediate reader-author relationship affected by the point to which Riley refers. For even if the reader is able to suspend not only his disbelief, but any consistent and rational understanding of the world in which the characters live, what can be the attitude of Sansón Carrasco, of the duke and duchess, of Antonio Moreno in Barcelona, of all the characters in the second part who have read the book and now meet the knight in his travels? The attitudes and activities of all of these characters in Part II are based upon a disbelief in enchanters, yet all accept the Don Quixote they meet as the same knight faithfully presented in the account of the Moorish enchanter.

10. "Arquitectura del *Quijote*," *Revista de Filología Española*, XXXII (1948), 283.
11. *Cervantes's Theory of the Novel*, p. 209.

If Don Quixote were to appear now at the door, could one accept him, and the novel as well? We are not dealing here with Hickock and Smith, in Capote's *In Cold Blood,* or Mailer's *Armies of the Night. Don Quixote* is a novel by an omniscient author, and is accepted *as such* by the characters in the second part. Surely we have passed through the looking glass into an impossible world. Américo Castro said in the article to which reference has already been made that Cervantes has presented us with "a play within a play, in such a subtle manner that it leaves in the reader the disturbing uncertainty of not knowing where one plane ends and the other begins."[12] We are in a position now to explain that "disturbing uncertainty." It arises from the unobtrusive, but nonetheless total, violation of the hitherto realistic world of the novel, through the intervention of an enchanter.

A poor writer might *tell* the reader that one's perspective conditions and distorts the perception of reality. A good writer could make the proposition *implicitly* evident in the relationships between the characters and their world. Cervantes seduces the reader into *acquiescing* in a wholly untenable perspective. Is not what Cervantes has accomplished here a sounder basis for the much discussed "perspectivism" in *Don Quixote* than the "basin-helmet" episode? Is it not much easier to identify with Don Quixote if one has, however superficially, shared his delusions? It may be objected that for Cervantes to make his point, the reader must become aware at some point that he has been fooled, and we have seen that the inverisimilitude is not usually perceived, but one has only to reread the quotation from Castro above to see that the "disturbing uncertainty" to which he refers arises precisely because the reader does not know just what has happened. Nor is Castro alone in this reaction to the novel. Others have noted that "one would not always need to have his head full of chivalric chimeras to wander off the road of reason,"[13] and decided that "the more one reads *Don Quixote* the more one

12. "Cervantes y Pirandello," p. 480.
13. Predmore, *The World of "Don Quixote,"* p. 31.

is driven to the conclusion that this mystification [about the nature of *Don Quixote*] is of Cervantes' own making. The author seems . . . to delight in pulling the wool over his readers' eyes."[14] In Chapter 1 we have seen how Cervantes' mystification about Don Quixote's real name and about the truth of the Cave of Montesinos episode produced a similar disorientation of the reader. Exposition of a proposition is outside, if not beneath, the art of the novel. Demonstration through action is the usual province of fiction. But *participation* on the reader's part is surely the highest aim of fiction, and this is clearly the effect of the situation we have been discussing.

Why does this total violation of the world of *Don Quixote* so often pass unnoticed by reader and critic alike? One can only conjecture. For one thing, the very profusion of levels discussed above probably lulls the reader into accepting yet another play within a play, without realizing that this case is radically different. For another, and this is the ultimate irony, *Don Quixote*, Part I, is the only specific object in the phenomenal world of Part II which exists literally, and lies ready at hand for our confirmation of its objective reality, yet it is precisely the presence of this book, *Don Quixote*, Part I, which violates the realistic terms of that world.

14. Bruce Wardropper, "The Pertinence of *El curioso impertinente*," *PMLA*, LXXII (1957), 588.

5. HERO OR FOOL?

Aristotle claimed that the tragic poet should be able to narrate his plot in simple form and produce, in reduced degree, the tragic emotions. . . . But suppose he wants his audience to pity what looks to any external view to be a wicked man, or to love, as in *Emma,* what looks to any external view to be a vain and meddling woman—what then? Why then all the rhetorical resources at his command . . . will be called in aid.

Wayne Booth, *The Rhetoric of Fiction,* p. 116.

We have seen the hand of Cervantes unobtrusively turn the reader from a systematically and painstakingly established attitude of derision, delighting in one deflation after another, to increased respect, sympathy, even admiration, in the progress of Part II. We had known that this evolution derived in part from such changes as Don Quixote's increasing cognizance of reality, his loss of control over events, the increase in deception practiced upon him, the element of self-doubt, and the shift from reliance upon physical prowess to reliance upon strength of spirit. But it is now evident, too, that Cervantes has guided the process throughout—not simply the changes in Don Quixote, but also our judgment of them: the reader has accepted the existence of a Moorish enchanter in the world of the novel since Part II, Chapter II; comic connotative displacement is no longer directed at the knight after Part II, Chapter X; chivalric archaism disappears from his speech after Part II, Chapter XXXII; the comic expectation of—and desire for—Don Quixote's defeat is consistently lacking after Part II, Chapter XLVIII.

These phenomena support some conclusions on extremely vexing problems of *Quixote* criticism. First, they are clear evidence that Cervantes does indeed direct the reader's ethical perspective toward Don Quixote. Second, they suggest that this guidance need not reflect some a priori ideological bias such as Hatzfeld, for example, ascribes to Cervantes:[1] "We

1. "Results from *Quijote* Criticism since 1947," p. 136. Hatzfeld has since remarked that those critics like himself who had categorized Cervantes' work as Baroque, basing their decision more upon form than ideology, were forced by Castro and his followers to "identify their own concept of Baroque with the expression of a specific ideology." *Estudios sobre el barroco* (Madrid, 1964), pp. 393-94.

are safe to assume that any chivalrous, pastoral, platonic and *alumbrado* attitude of Don Quijote is criticized by the realistic, anti-romantic, Aristotelian and Tridentine Cervantes." Don Quixote's error is much more human, more individual *and* more universal at the same time: the sin of pride.

We have seen the sin; we have better understood the laughter provoked as justice exacted its punishment, but we have not examined the extent and variety of the reader's reactions to the changes in Don Quixote and in Cervantes' ethical orientation. In the ten chapters from Part II (LVIII-LXVIII) which we have called crucial (page 47) in the shift of reader sympathy, an important note is that of pity for Don Quixote. In Part I, the theme of pity appeared but briefly, following the speech on Arms and Letters. It is Don Quixote himself who first mentions pity in Part II, and he makes the reader aware of how painful it will be for a man who sees himself as he does to find himself the object of this emotion. He closes his letter to Sancho with this phrase: "I commend you to God, and may He keep you from becoming an object of pity to anyone" (846). The Castilian who berates Don Quixote in the streets of Barcelona concludes his remarks with the comment that "it is a very great pity to see the good sense they say the fool displays on all other subjects drained off like this through the channel of his knight-errantry" (917). Don Quixote does not even reply. Finally, Sansón Carrasco, in explaining to Don Antonio the reason for his imposture as the Knight of the White Moon, remarks that Don Quixote's "madness and absurdities inspire pity in all of us who know him" (938).

But what of the other tragic emotion? To produce fear in the reader, Cervantes must achieve more than sympathy for his protagonist. He must seduce the reader into a feeling of identification with Don Quixote's strivings, for without identification, the impending disaster and ethical crisis of Part II will produce only "a kind of faint alarm which is the comic analogue of fear."[2] Can one identify with Don Quixote in the

2. Ronald S. Crane, "The Plot of *Tom Jones*," in *Essays on the*

comic failings which result from undisciplined egocentricity, *and* in the tragic failure of undeniably heroic aspirations, which are continually vitiated by the same central weakness?

The prime heroic ingredient in the confrontation with reality in *Don Quixote* is faith, and the expression of this faith in commitment. The early episode with the Toledan silk merchants lays the cornerstone for this foundation of Don Quixote's character. At the knight's demand that they affirm the absolute supremacy of Dulcinea's beauty, the merchants ask that he show them a portrait of the lady, even one no bigger than a grain of wheat, "in order that we may not have upon our consciences the burden of confessing a thing which we have never seen nor heard" (46). Don Quixote states his position as follows: "The important thing is for you, *without seeing her,* to believe, confess, affirm, swear, and defend that truth" (45). This stance is precisely in accord with Saint Paul's definition of faith: "Now faith is the assurance of things hoped for, the conviction of things not seen" (Hebrews 11:1). The culmination of Don Quixote's witness to the faith of which Dulcinea is the embodiment is, of course, his acquiescence in martyrdom at the hands of the Knight of the White Moon.

The introduction of the innkeeper who believes in the historical truth of the novels of chivalry offers a needed distinction between committed faith and simple belief. The curate chides him for his credulity, saying: "Please God you do not go lame on the same foot as your guest Don Quixote." The innkeeper's response is significant: "That I shall not. I could never be so mad as to turn knight-errant, for I am aware that the customs of those days when famous knights roamed the world no longer prevail today" (279). The innkeeper is content to affirm the truth of the novels of chivalry; Don Quixote must witness to it.[3] One is reminded of an exchange in *Waiting for Godot*:

Eighteenth Century Novel, ed. R. D. Spector (Bloomington, 1965), p. 121.

3. Cf. Jorge Mañach, *Examen del quijotismo* (Buenos Aires, 1950), p. 128, and Casalduero, *Sentido y forma del "Quijote,"* p. 153.

VLADIMIR: But you can't go barefoot!

ESTRAGON: Christ did.

VLADIMIR: Christ! What has Christ got to do with it? You're not going to compare yourself to Christ!

ESTRAGON: All my life I've compared myself to him.

VLADIMIR: But where he lived it was warm, it was dry.

ESTRAGON: Yes. And they crucified quick.[4]

"Chivalry is a religion in itself" (561), was Don Quixote's reply to Sancho's suggestion that they seek sainthood rather than follow knight-errantry, and the knight's answer to the barber's question about the giant Morgante's stature should remind the reader that the difference between one faith and another is as nothing compared to the conflict between faith and reason: " 'On this subject of giants,' replied the knight, 'opinions differ as to whether or not there ever were any in this world: but the Holy Scriptures, which do not depart from the truth by one iota, show us plainly that giants did exist' " (519).

In this connection the "Story of the One Who Was Too Curious for His Own Good" serves as a negative apologue (a principal function of the digression in *Tom Jones,* according to Sacks[5]) to the problem of faith and reason as presented in the novel as a whole. Anselmo has taken the path of strict rational empiricism, and he cannot be sure of the chastity of Camila, "until the quality of her virtue is proved to me in the same manner that fire brings out the purity of gold" (283). Lotario draws the distinction between reason and faith in terms of Moors and Christians, comparing Anselmo in his sinful condition to the former: "It seems to me that you are reasoning now as the Moors always do, who cannot be brought

4. Samuel Beckett, *Waiting for Godot* (New York, 1954), p. 35.

5. *Fiction and the Shape of Belief*: an apologue, for Sacks, is "organized as a fictional example of the truth of a formulable statement or closely related set of such statements" (p. 8), and in *Tom Jones* "the controlling ideas of the apologues are made relevant as ethical comment on the actions of the important characters in the novel" (p. 228).

to see the error inherent in their sect, through citations from Holy Writ; nor are they to be moved by intellectual speculation or arguments based upon the articles of faith, but they demand *palpable examples,* readily understood and demonstrable, and such as admit of undeniable and indubitable mathematical proof. . . . it has to be shown them with the hands and placed before their eyes . . ." (285). Cervantes has included the "Story of the One Who Was Too Curious for His Own Good" to show clearly that this attitude is not the answer to the problems of existence, and therefore that Don Quixote's failure is not the result of his credulity—that his inadequacy is more serious than an inability to demythologize the novels of chivalry—while at the same time underlining the fact that he is eminently a man of faith.

But the problem so skillfully drawn by Cervantes in *Don Quixote* is not the adequacy of the faith, nor its applicability in the real world. Saint Paul reminded the Corinthians that they were called to be "fools for Christ" (I Corinthians 4:10). The problem here is the purity of the believer, not the belief, and Part II is the process of purification through which Don Quixote must pass to restabilize his relations with the world. He returns home "victor over himself," and his return to sanity is but an epilogue to the real transformation. Impending disaster for Don Quixote in Part II produces fear in the reader to the extent that his own beliefs are analogous to Don Quixote's, and, more importantly, insofar as his own inadequacy and presumption in adhering to them are reflected in Don Quixote. To clarify the archetypal trajectory of the life of Don Quixote it may be useful to juxtapose relevant quotations from the novel with a paraphrase of Kirkegaard's three essential stages of human existence:

Once the individual has passed beyond the *aesthetic* stage on life's way, has outgrown merely dreaming over and enjoying life . . .	The aforesaid gentleman, on those occasions when he was at leisure, which was most of the year around, was in the habit of reading books of chivalry with such pleasure and devotion as to

he plunges into the midst of things, he commits himself and becomes involved (*engagé*) at the *ethical* level. . . . He takes sides in the great struggle between right and wrong, assuming his burden as a finite being who submits to an infinite requirement.

Yet in the process of this striving the individual becomes increasingly aware of his own and others' failures in comparison with what ought to be, the perfect, the infinite demand. Painful awareness grows of how far he and mankind in general fall short of the ideal.

The individual acquires a deepening sense of wrongdoing, weakness, distress, and a desire for repentance.

At the close of this second stage, a man comes to know himself as a *guilty* being. . . . The ethical stage culminates in repentance.

There is a yearning for something further that shall lead us beyond the world of natural existence. Such an attitude of despondency at not finding what we sought . . . leads to transition

lead him almost wholly to forget the life of a hunter and even the administration of his estate(26).

It now appeared to him fitting and necessary . . . to become a knight-errant . . . he would right every manner of wrong, placing himself in situations of the greatest peril such as would redound to the eternal glory of his name (27).

Up to now, I do not know what I have won with all the hardships I have endured. However, if my lady Dulcinea were but free of those she is suffering, it may be that my fortunes would improve, and with a sounder mind I should be able to tread a better path than the one I follow at present (884). Today, owing to the state of sin in which we live, idleness and sloth, gluttony and luxury, rule triumphant (624).

Each man is the architect of his own fortune. I was the architect of mine, but I did not observe the necessary prudence, and as a result my presumptuousness has brought me to a sorry end (943).

Those profane stories dealing with knight-errantry are odious to me, and I realize how foolish I was and the danger I courted in reading them (984).

"Say no more, in Heaven's name, but be sensible and forget these idle tales."

"Tales of that kind," said Don Quixote, "have been the truth for me in the past, and to my detrito the third level of the *reli-gious,* with its awareness of an eternal power permeating existence.[6]

ment, but with Heaven's aid I trust to turn them to my profit now that I am dying" (984-85).

Those who say that Cervantes does not attack Don Quixote's faith are right, for this is the lesson of the "Story of the One Who Was Too Curious for His Own Good." Those who say that he is a hero are right, for he dies "victor over himself" by renouncing his egocentric blindness. Those who say that Cervantes does not attack chivalric idealism are right, for Don Quixote is victor over himself *before* he renounces chivalry. On the other hand, those who say that Don Quixote is the butt of Cervantes' satire are right, for his egotism is ludicrous, and we have seen how Cervantes' systematic emphasis on the knight's pride permits one to laugh at his expense. Those who say that Don Quixote's mission was a failure are right, but not because it was crushed by an unworthy world—since the defeats were presented as deserved—nor because the *mission* was foolish.[7] Witness the initial reaction of Diego de Miranda to Don Quixote's mission: "I find it hard to convince myself that at the present time there is anyone on earth who goes about aiding widows, protecting damsels, defending the honor of wives, and succoring orphans, and I should never have believed it had I not beheld

6. Marie Collins Swabey, *Comic Laughter. A Philosophical Essay* (New Haven and London, 1961), pp. 94-95.

7. Manuel Durán, in *La ambigüedad en el "Quijote,"* seems to sustain the rightness of both sides of this controversy when he says that "the way in which Don Quijote tries to apply chivalric ideals may be laughable; but the personality of the hero captivates the reader. . . . Thus it is that the 'hard critics' and the 'soft' ones are equally correct, since the two aspects—criticism of certain activity and the creation of an admirable character who is in turn the source of the criticized activity—coexist in the novel" (p. 130), but he still sees the flaw as somehow external: "The interior, chivalric image turns out to be inadequate and clumsy in its relations with external [reality]" (p. 132), and again: "The hero is thus at the same time attractive and admirable, since he has managed to forge an ideal by virtue of which he organizes his world, but also worthy of pity or blame, since this ideal does not prove compatible with the life of the collectivity" (p. 256). Pity would certainly be appropriate, if this were the essential situation; *blame* would seem less justifiable, and *laughter*, so frequently called forth, would seem little short of incomprehensible.

your Grace with my own eyes. Thank Heaven for that book that your Grace tells me has been published concerning your true and exalted deeds of chivalry, as it should cast into oblivion all the innumerable stories of fictitious knights-errant with which the world is filled, greatly to the detriment of good morals and the prejudice and discredit of legitimate histories" (606).

What is the object of Cervantes' satire? Outside the book it is *bad novels* of chivalry, criticized primarily for defective style and lack of verisimilitude. Within the novel, it is Don Quixote's undisciplined egocentricity, and Part II is the story of his recovery. If a man's life is a work of art, Don Quixote must correct in *his* life the same defects which disturb Cervantes in the novels of chivalry: a presumptuous and altisonant style, and lack of concordance with reality. Of course Cervantes is only Don Quixote's "stepfather" (11), since every man "is the son of his works" (43).

The arrogant "I know who I am" (49) of Don Quixote's first sally is as empty as Segismundo's "I know who I am" in Calderón's *Life Is a Dream*.[8] Both men speak these words at the moment of greatest self-deception, and both are brought by a process of *desengaño*—Baroque disillusionment —to the same realization: "Today my greatest triumph is the victory I've won over myself."[9]

> "Not so fast, gentlemen," said Don Quixote. "In last year's nests there are no birds this year. I was mad and now I am sane; I was Don Quixote de la Mancha, and now I am, as I have said, Alonso Quijano the Good. May my repentance and the truth I now speak restore me to the place I once held in your esteem" (986).

8. Pedro Calderón de la Barca, *Life Is a Dream*, trans. William E. Colford (Great Neck, N.Y., 1958), II. vi.
9. *Life Is a Dream*, III. xiv.

UNIVERSITY OF FLORIDA MONOGRAPHS

Humanities

No. 1: *Uncollected Letters of James Gates Percival,* edited by Harry R. Warfel

No. 2: *Leigh Hunt's Autobiography: The Earliest Sketches,* edited by Stephen F. Fogle

No. 3: *Pause Patterns in Elizabethan and Jacobean Drama,* by Ants Oras

No. 4: *Rhetoric and American Poetry of the Early National Period,* by Gordon E. Bigelow

No. 5: *The Background of The Princess Casamassima,* by W. H. Tilley

No. 6: *Indian Sculpture in the John and Mable Ringling Museum of Art,* by Roy C. Craven, Jr.

No. 7: *The Cestus. A Mask,* edited by Thomas B. Stroup

No. 8: *Tamburlaine, Part I, and Its Audience,* by Frank B. Fieler

No. 9: *The Case of John Darrell: Minister and Exorcist,* by Corinne Holt Rickert

No. 10: *Reflections of the Civil War in Southern Humor,* by Wade H. Hall

No. 11: *Charles Dodgson, Semeiotician,* by Daniel F. Kirk

No. 12: *Three Middle English Religious Poems,* edited by R. H. Bowers

No. 13: *The Existentialism of Miguel de Unamuno,* by José Huertas-Jourda

No. 14: *Four Spiritual Crises in Mid-Century American Fiction,* by Robert Detweiler

No. 15: *Style and Society in German Literary Expressionism,* by Egbert Krispyn

No. 16: *The Reach of Art: A Study in the Prosody of Pope,* by Jacob H. Adler

No. 17: *Malraux, Sartre, and Aragon as Political Novelists,* by Catharine Savage

No. 18: *Las Guerras Carlistas y el Reinado Isabelino en la Obra de Ramón del Valle-Inclán,* por María Dolores Lado

No. 19: *Diderot's Vie de Sénèque: A Swan Song Revised,* by Douglas A. Bonneville

No. 20: *Blank Verse and Chronology in Milton,* by Ants Oras

No. 21: *Milton's Elisions,* by Robert O. Evans

No. 22: *Prayer in Sixteenth-Century England,* by Faye L. Kelly

No. 23: *The Strangers: The Tragic World of Tristan L'Hermite,* by Claude K. Abraham

No. 24: *Dramatic Uses of Biblical Allusion in Marlowe and Shakespeare,* by James H. Sims

No. 25: *Doubt and Dogma in Maria Edgeworth,* by Mark D. Hawthorne

No. 26: *The Masses of Francesco Soriano,* by S. Philip Kniseley

No. 27: *Love as Death in The Iceman Cometh,* by Winifred Dusenbury Frazer

No. 28: *Melville and Authority,* by Nicholas Canaday, Jr.

No. 29: *Don Quixote: Hero or Fool? A Study in Narrative Technique,* by John J. Allen

DATE DUE

WITHDRAWN